SUCCESSFUL INDOOR GARDENING

EXOTIC
ORCHIDS

SUCCESSFUL INDOOR GARDENING

EXOTIC
ORCHIDS

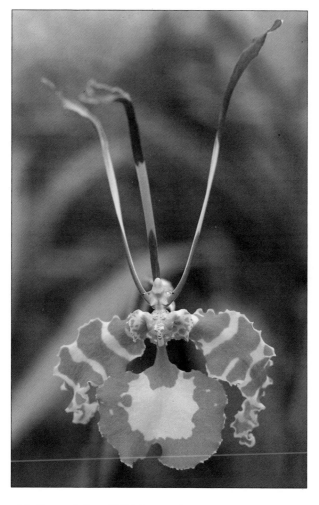

Edited by Wilma Rittershausen

HPBooks
a division of
PRICE STERN SLOAN
Los Angeles

A Salamander Book

Published by HPBooks, a division of Price Stern Sloan, Inc.
360 North La Cienega Boulevard, Los Angeles, California 90048.
Printed in Belgium.

9 8 7 6 5 4 3 2 1

Key to abbreviations

AM   Award of Merit
RHS   Royal Horticultural Society
GMM   George Moore Medal

Library of Congress Cataloging-in-Publication Data

Rittershausen, Wilma.
    Exotic orchids.

    (Successful indoor gardening)
    Includes index.
    1. Orchids.   2. Orchid culture.   I. Title.   II. Series.
SB409.W57   1989   635.9'3415   89-2015
ISBN 0-89586-833-4

Credits

Introduction written by: David Squire
Editors: Wilma Rittershausen and Geoffrey Rogers
Assistant editor: Lisa Dyer
Designer: Rod Ferring
Photographer: Eric Crichton
Line artwork: David Leigh
Typeset by: Gee Graphics Ltd.
Color separation by: Magnum Graphics Ltd.
Printed by: Proost International Book Production, Turnhout, Belgium

Contents

Introduction	6
Easy to Grow	14
Moderately Easy to Grow	68
Difficult to Grow	84
Index	95

Introduction

Few plants create such an aura of mystique and grandeur as orchids. Their delicate, intricate, colourful and often waxy appearance has enthralled many people. Indeed, just to mention orchids can arouse thoughts of flowers which, to many people, are considered as the elite of the plant world. It should be emphasized though that orchids are challenging plants to grow and you do require a greenhouse or conservatory if you are to cultivate them successfully.

This informative guide features over 75 of the more exotic varieties of orchid. The comprehensive growing instructions include such essential information as the resting and temperature requirements of each plant and to help you choose which species will best suit you, according to your experience and success rate, the plants have been grouped into three sections – easy to grow, moderately easy to grow and difficult to grow.

The orchid family

The orchid family is one of the largest in the plant kingdom, having about 750 different genera with at least 25,000 native species and more than 30,000 cultivated hybrids – the result of interbreeding – and more are being produced each year.

There are two basic types of orchids: the *terrestrial* species which grow at ground level and are rooted in the soil, and the *epiphytic* types which grow on trees and shrubs. The native terrestrial types grow mainly in temperate regions, while the epiphytic forms are chiefly found in tropical or sub-tropical areas, where their frequently

Above: Even within one group of orchids, the slipper orchids (Paphiopedilum), the range of flower *shapes, sizes and colours is wide. These orchids are easy to grow indoors in draught-free rooms.*

The Flower Parts of a Cymbidium Orchid

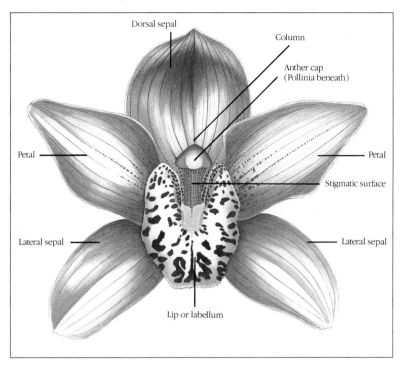

Dorsal sepal

Column

Anther cap
(Pollinia beneath)

Petal

Petal

Stigmatic surface

Lateral sepal

Lateral sepal

Lip or labellum

exposed roots will not be damaged. Although the epiphytic types grow above soil-level on the branches and shoots of trees and shrubs, they are not parasites. They do not take food from their hosts, merely using them as support and anchorage. They usually grow in dead plant debris which collects in the angles of branches, as well as in the crevices of bark. Their roots draw nourishment and moisture from this debris. Some epiphytic orchids grow on rocks and are more correctly termed lithophytes. Epiphytic orchids usually have showier, larger and more flamboyant flowers than the terrestrial types, and it is therefore from these species that most of the cultivated and hybridized forms are selected and derived.

Native terrestrial orchids are usually not so abundant as other wild flowers, and in recent years they have become even scarcer as land has been developed for road, industrial and habitation purposes – as well as by the indiscriminate and irresponsible behaviour of some wild flower enthusiasts. Therefore, if you do find orchids in the wild, do not pick the flowers or dig up the plants. Just take a picture of them and tell a local natural history society of their whereabouts.

Orchid flowers
The flowers range in size from minute types, which demand the use of a magnifying lens to appreciate their beauty, to those up to 20cm (8in) wide. Even within a genus their size and shape vary considerably, although all orchids are basically the same. Each has three sepals (the outermost segments of a flower) and three petals. All of these are coloured, whereas in many flowers the sepals are green and leaf-like. The uppermost sepal is symmetrical and often slightly larger than the other two. Its size varies from species to species, and plant breeders have developed plants with larger and more distinctive sepals. The petals on either side of a flower are usually equal in size and shape, whereas the bottom one is formed into the shape of a lip and known as the labellum. It is the most ornamental of all the flower parts of an orchid and acts as a landing platform for pollinating insects.

Getting the Best from Orchids

Orchids need special treatment although, despite their often delicate and exotic appearance, many are easily grown and are remarkably tolerant of neglect. Many can be encouraged to flower indoors, but during their dormant period a conservatory or greenhouse is essential.

Resting period Many orchids have a summer growing season followed by a winter resting period. When at rest, all growth stops and the plant uses the reserves stored in its pseudobulbs. A resting orchid should be placed in full light and kept mostly dry until new growth is seen. A plant about to rest may shed some or all of its foliage, depending on whether it is an evergreen, deciduous or semi-deciduous type.

Compost The specific mixture needed varies betwen genera. Proprietary compost mixtures specifically for epiphytic orchids are available, but a mixture of moist peat, finely ground bark, sphagnum moss and vermiculite is also suitable. Terrestrial orchids need a compost with a higher loam content, and one of equal parts fibrous loam, moist peat, sharp sand and sphagnum moss is required.

Potting Plants should be kept in as small a pot as possible, with repotting taking place after flowering or when new growth and roots are appearing. If the plant is being newly potted, place the rhizome on a good layer of drainage material and then add compost all around. The crown must be left level with the pot's rim, and if aerial roots are present they should be left outside the pot. With established plants, remove the plant from its pot and carefully tease away the old compost. Cut off the dead roots, then pack fresh compost around the remaining roots; this is best done by holding the plant upside down and packing compost around and between the roots to form a small mound. Now place the pot on top, turn both pot and plant the right way up and pack more compost around the plant. Some epiphytic orchids, because of their growth or flowering habits, are best grown in slatted wood baskets or on rafts of wood. Allow a week to pass before watering newly-potted orchids, and then water them only sparingly for about two weeks until the plant is established in its new pot.

Below: When new roots appear, most orchids can be repotted. You can also repot after flowering.

Below: Epiphytic orchids can be grown on rafts of wood, bound in place over a pad of sphagnum moss.

Watering When the orchid is growing the compost must be kept moist. Terrestrial orchids can be watered by gently trickling water onto the the surface of the compost, but with epiphytic types you should plunge the whole plant and its container into a bucket of water every three or four days during summer; at other times and when the weather is cooler do this only once a week.

Feeding Many orchids can soon be killed by excessive feeding. The information given on each species indicates if it is safe to feed a specific plant. In the appropriate instances, feeding should be carried out during late spring and summer.

Humidity Orchids need a humid atmosphere, especially in summer. Lightly mist spray plants in summer, preferably three or more times a day. Trays of pebbles and water, as well as misting below the staging in greenhouses and on floors, also helps to increase the general level of humidity, but remember that the plants also need a good supply of fresh air.

Temperatures Orchids can be classified into three types according to the temperatures they require:
☐ Cool types need a minimum winter night temperature of 10°C (50°F) rising to a maximum summer day temperature of 24°C (75°F), with an average growing temperature between these depending on the season and the immediate weather.
☐ Intermediate types need a minimum winter night temperature of 13°C (55°F), with a similar growing average and maximum temperature as the cool types.
☐ Warm types require no less than 18°C (64°F) as a winter night minimum, and are often better with 21°C (70°F). This should rise by at least 5°C (10°F) during the day.
For each plant in this book, the type has been indicated, together with the minimum night temperature during winter.

Shade Orchids are shade-loving plants. From early spring to the end of summer you should shade the plants, preferably with slatted wooden blinds. For the rest of the year allow light to reach them as, in moderation, light is needed to ripen the resting plants.

Below: Orchids grown in greenhouses benefit from shade created by slatted wooden blinds, which can be rolled down during hot weather. Wire-mesh staging allows fresh air to circulate.

Displaying Orchids Indoors

Orchids are normally grown in conservatories or greenhouses but, when in flower, many can be taken indoors. Indeed, to leave a superbly-flowered orchid in a greenhouse is rather a waste when it can perhaps be better displayed – and to many more admirers – inside the home.

Orchids in containers Orchids grown in pots, as well as those in slatted wooden baskets, need to be placed in attractive cache pots or even larger, ornate tubs on legs which can hold several pots at a time. Because the air indoors is relatively dry – and it is impossible to mist spray the plants and their surroundings in the same free manner as in a conservatory or greenhouse – stand the pots on a layer of pebbles, and keep the pebbles permanently moist. Ideally, you should pack moist peat between the growing pot and the cache pot. Ensure, however, that this does not encourage water to lay in the bottom of the cache pot which will then make the compost in the growing pot too wet and cold.

If you have an ornate wooden tub, but do not wish the inside to become saturated with water, line it with plastic – a dustbin (trash can) liner is useful for this purpose. Finely-leaved foliage plants, such as some ferns, can be used in combination with orchids, helping to create a more humid micro-climate. Choose the additional plants carefully, as they should complement and highlight the orchids without dominating them.

Choosing the right position indoors is important. Warm areas above fireplaces and radiators are certain death traps for orchids, as the plants soon become dry and the arid air shrivels the leaves and flowers. Orchids dislike strong sunlight, so do not place them on windowsills. Conversely, do not choose a dark position, one with rapidly fluctuating temperatures or one that is draughty. East-facing windowsills can be used, but take care to move the plants further into the room at night if the window does not have double-glazing. And never trap plants between the window and a drawn curtain.

Orchids indoors invariably need more frequent watering than those in a greenhouse. Because, when watering epiphytic types, the compost needs to be thoroughly soaked, take the plant to the kitchen and immerse the compost in a bowl of water. Allow the pot to drain thoroughly before replacing it in its flowering position.

Orchids in vases Instead of taking the whole plant indoors, flower spikes can be cut off and displayed in vases. When the last flower on a spike has been open for two or three weeks, the plant benefits from the spike being cut off, but you should not cut off the spike until the terminal flower has been open for at least ten days.

Place the spike in clean water and provide a cool position, out of direct sunlight and away from cold draughts. This way, the flower spike will last as long off the plant as when left on. Every few days, cut a thin slice off the bottom of the flower stem and renew the water. Cut the base of the stem at a slant, so that the largest possible area of stem is exposed to absorb water. Do not crush the base of the stem, as this blocks the water passages and shortens the life of the flowers.

Buttonholes and corsages Some orchids combine with other plants to create superb buttonholes and corsages. A distinctive dendrobium or phalaenopsis orchid, combined with the sweetly-scented flowering houseplant stephanotis and a few variegated leaves from foliage houseplants create an eye-catching feature. To make a corsage, in addition to the flowers and the foliage, you will need a length of fine wire and some green florists' tape. Before using the orchids in the display, place them in water overnight. This increases the period for which the flowers remain fresh. If, when completed, the corsage is placed in a plastic box and put in a refrigerator it will remain in good condition for several days.

Below left: Special display cases such as this are ideal for growing orchids indoors. The cabinets are fitted with growth-inducing fluorescent tubes.

Below: An orchid combined with a few leaves makes an attractive corsage. Wire each component individually, bind the wires together then cover them with tape.

Good Health Guide

Orchids, like all other plants, are likely to be attacked by pests or diseases at some time during their lives. Slight infestations are likely to achieve epidemic proportions if not treated quickly. Therefore, vigilance and a rapid response to signs of pests and diseases are essential. Regular monthly spraying with a systemic insecticide is recommended as a way to prevent a serious build up of pests.

Pests which infest orchids
- **Aphids**, often known as greenfly, cluster in soft parts of a plant, especially around shoot tips. They are green, plumpish and may have wings. They emit a sticky honeydew, which may become covered with black, sooty mould. To kill these pests, use a systemic insecticide.
- **Red spider mites** are minute, straw-coloured or brownish-red spiders' which infest orchids. False spider mites have recently become troublesome on a few orchids, causing pitting on the upper surfaces of the leaves. Both of these spiders are difficult to eradicate, but regular sprayings with a systemic insecticide will keep them under control.
- **Mealy bugs** are slow-moving – eventually static – pests which resemble small, woolly woodlice. They cluster beneath leaves, in leaf joints and on buds, sucking sap and emitting sticky honeydew which encourages the presence of sooty mould. The pests can be killed off with a systemic insecticide.
- **Scale insects** are brown disc-like pests – some soft, others hard – which cause pale spots on leaves and are difficult to eradicate. Use a systemic insecticide as soon as they are seen. Fresh colonies can be wiped off leaves by using a damp cotton bud.
- **Weevils** are like small beetles which attack and chew roots, as well as stems, leaves and flowers. They are usually nocturnal feeders, hiding during the day. If they attack roots, compost-drenching chemicals can be used. If above compost-level, spray the plant with a general insecticide. Always check the roots for this pest when repotting your orchids.
- **Thrips** are fast-moving, fly-like pests which feed on flowers and leaves by piercing the tissue and sucking. They cause silvery mottling and prevent normal flower and leaf development. Regularly applied systemic insecticides help to control them.

Diseases which attack orchids
- **Petal blight** is a fungal disease which results in dark brown or black spots, with pinkish margins, on the petals. It occurs mainly on the early autumn flowers of phalaenopsis and cattleya orchids. Remove infected flowers and ensure that the night-time humidity is not too high. In cool situations, give additional warmth in autumn to prevent the problem arising.
- **Brown spot** is a bacterial disease which occurs mainly in phalaenopsis and paphiopedilum orchids. Early signs of infection are soft and watery areas on leaves which quickly turn brown. Infected areas must be cut out as soon as they are noticed and the cut surfaces dusted with a fungicide.
- **Virus diseases** enter the tissues of plants and are difficult – if not impossible – to eradicate. They are frequently spread by sucking pests such as aphids. It is therefore essential to be vigilant and to prevent any pest infestation spreading. The symptoms of viruses are wide and depend not only on the virus but the plant as well.

Weak and badly-grown plants show signs of attack at an early stage. Mottling, irregular stripes and blotches of different colours are all symptoms.

Cymbidium mosaic virus attacks most parts of a plant and infects all orchids. Regrettably, there is no cure. Discoloured areas occur on leaves, becoming darker and sunken as the disease spreads. These sometimes form a diamond pattern. On phalaenopsis and cattleya orchids the infection reveals itself initially as purplish markings which, within a few weeks, become brown.

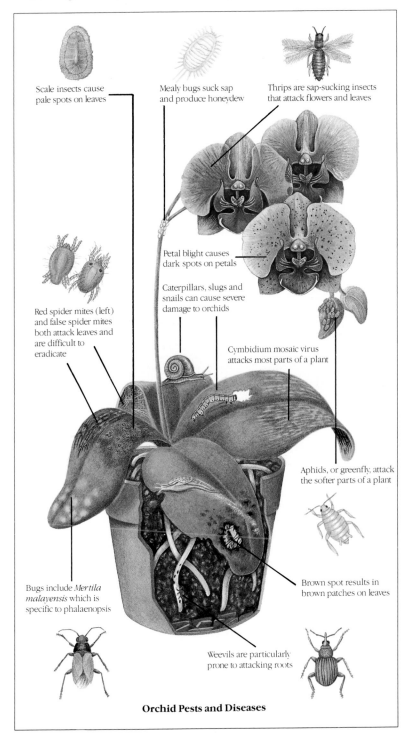

Scale insects cause pale spots on leaves

Mealy bugs suck sap and produce honeydew

Thrips are sap-sucking insects that attack flowers and leaves

Petal blight causes dark spots on petals

Red spider mites (left) and false spider mites both attack leaves and are difficult to eradicate

Caterpillars, slugs and snails can cause severe damage to orchids

Cymbidium mosaic virus attacks most parts of a plant

Aphids, or greenfly, attack the softer parts of a plant

Bugs include *Mertila malayensis* which is specific to phalaenopsis

Brown spot results in brown patches on leaves

Weevils are particularly prone to attacking roots

Orchid Pests and Diseases

Easy to Grow

Orchids have always been thought to be difficult to grow, and in general they are. There are some, however, which are ideal for newly-inspired growers of orchids, being easier to grow and to flower than other varieties. Many of the orchids described in this section do not demand excessively warm conditions, which make them even more suitable for beginners. Some of them need a resting period, while others do not.

Among the easy-to-grow orchids are some which are ideally suited to indoor flowering. These include many orchids which belong to the genera Paphiopedilum and Phalaenopsis, as well as those Cattleyas which have been crossed with Sophronitis and Laelias to produce smaller-growing plants with a large flowers-to-plant ratio.

Ada aurantiaca

This species belongs to an extremely small genus of only three species, which are allied to the odontoglossums. It is an epiphyte from Colombia, where it grows in the same location as many of the odontoglossums and therefore requires similar cool house conditions. Although *Ada aurantiaca* is allied to odontoglossums, very little hybridizing has been achieved and the species is grown for its unusually brilliant orange flowers, which appear on compact sprays during the winter and spring. The individual blooms are small and are not fully opening, but produce bell-shaped flowers which are most attractive on the spray.

The plant is a neat, compact grower that can be easily raised from seed and is therefore plentiful. It produces small pseudobulbs, which are partially protected by the base of the outside leaves. The flower spike comes from the base of the leading bulb when it has completed its growth. Pot in an open, well-drained bark compost. Do not overpot. Best when grown on without division.

- ☐ Cool: 10°C (50°F)
- ☐ Winter/spring flowering
- ☐ Evergreen/no rest

Left: Ada aurantiaca is a cool-growing species which blooms in the winter and spring. It flowers best when the roots are constricted in the pot. Do not pot on too frequently.

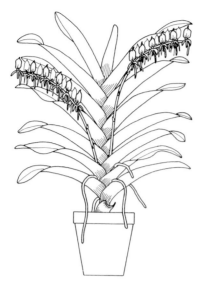

12 flowers about 10cm (4in) in diameter. The sepals, petals and spur are green and the lip pure white. Curiously, the flowers appear on the stem as if upside-down.

The plant thrives in generous conditions and should be watered throughout the year. During the summer months regular overhead spraying of the foliage and aerial roots is beneficial. The plant can also be foliar fed in the same way for nine months of the year. Although it likes a position in good light, the leaves are all too easily burnt if it is allowed to stand in bright sunlight for any length of time. A good position for this plant is near to the glass (which should be shaded in summer) suspended in a hanging basket. Not suited to indoor culture.

Angraecum eburneum

There are over 200 species of angraecums, although very few are seen in cultivation. They come mainly from tropical Africa.

This winter-flowering species resembles *Angraecum sesquipedale* in plant habit but the flower spikes are often longer, producing nine to

☐ Warm: 18°C (65°F)
☐ Winter flowering
☐ Evergreen/no rest

Below: Angraecum eburneum is a large species well suited for a warm environment. Long sprays of fragrant flowers are produced during the winter.

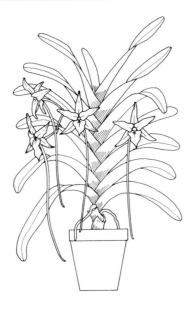

arise from the leaf axils, are 15-18cm (6-7in) across and a beautiful creamy-white in colour. Their most distinctive feature is a greenish spur that may be up to 30cm (12in) in length. The flowers appear in the winter months. They are long lasting on the plant and very fragrant.

Even though this epiphytic genus is restricted to parts of Africa and the island of Madagascar, some 200 species are known.

Angraecums are subjects for the warm house, and being without pseudobulbs require moist conditions and plenty of light. However, some of the smaller-growing plants should be protected from full sun, and for all plants frequent spraying can be a great advantage for healthy growth.

Angraecum sesquipedale

This is the best-known of the large angraecums and produces one of the most majestic of all orchid flowers. The plant, which can grow to a height of 90cm (36in), has strap-like leathery leaves that equal the plant's height in span. The star-shaped flowers, produced two to four on stems that

☐ Warm 18°C (65°F)
☐ Winter flowering
☐ Evergreen/no rest

Below: A magnificent species for the warm greenhouse, Angraecum sesquipedale requires good light. The large waxy flowers appear during the winter months.

Anguloa clowesii

Below: The beautiful, cool-growing Anguloa clowesii, commonly known as the 'cradle orchid', blooms in early summer.

Anguloa is a small genus of about ten species which grow naturally as epiphytes and terrestrials. They are high altitude plants from South America.

This large and beautiful species is commonly known as the 'cradle orchid' owing to the ability of the lip, which is loosely hinged, to rock back and forth when tilted. The lip is fully enclosed by the rest of the flower, which gives rise to a further popular name of 'tulip orchid'. The plant will grow well with lycastes but is considerably larger when in leaf.

Plenty of water and feed should be given during the growing season, when the plant is making up its large pseudobulbs. Water should be withheld when the leaves are shed at the end of the growing season. The flowers, 7.5cm (3in) across, appear singly from a stout stem at the same time as the new growth. They are a lovely canary yellow with a strong fragrance.

This lovely orchid originates from Colombia and today nursery-raised plants are usually available. Suitable for cool greenhouse culture.

- ☐ Cool: 11°C (52°F)
- ☐ Early summer flowering
- ☐ Deciduous/rest in winter

Above: An easily grown species for the cool house, Bifrenaria harrisoniae requires good light. It flowers during the summer.

Bifrenaria harrisoniae

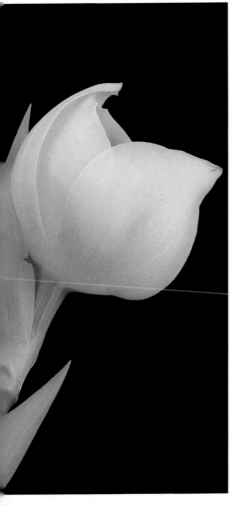

This is the most familiar species of the *Bifrenaria* genus. It produces creamy-white flowers, one or two to a stem, with thick waxy sepals and petals and a lip covered with short, reddish-purple hairs. Each flower can be up to 7.5cm (3in) in diameter.

It belongs to a small genus of about a dozen species, coming mainly from Brazil. They are certainly among the easiest of plants to grow, and are often offered in collections for beginners.

Although they are usually grown in the intermediate house, with plenty of light, they will also do well in the cool house with a winter minimum of 11°C (52°F). Bifrenarias are epiphytic and will succeed if grown in a pot on the staging, or in wire or wooden baskets suspended from the roof; they should be kept drier at the root when not in active growth. An open compost with good drainage is important.

Allow the plant a complete rest during the winter, giving no water until the new growth is seen to appear during the very early spring. Propagation is a slow process.

☐ Cool: 11°C (52°F)
☐ Early summer flowering
☐ Evergreen/dry rest

During the winter it requires slightly less water than in the summer months, but it should not be allowed to dry out so that the pseudobulbs shrivel. The sweetly fragrant flowers are carried on graceful sprays of up to a dozen blooms during the early summer. The sepals and   petals are curiously long and narrow, which gives rise to the plant's common name of 'spider orchid'. This characteristic gives the flowers a lovely light and wispy appearance. The colour is light green with darker green spotting.

This plant will often 'climb' out of its pot and is a good subject for mounting on wood, when long aerial roots are produced. An ideal orchid for beginners.

Although about 30 species of this genus are known, only a very few are still grown.

Brassia verrucosa

This is one of the most popular of the brassias, a genus of epiphytic orchids from South America. They are allied to, and will interbreed with, plants from the odontoglossum group. *B. verrucosa* is a neat, compact grower that will do well indoors or in a cool greenhouse.

☐ Cool: 10°C (50°F)
☐ Early summer flowering
☐ Evergreen/semi-rest

Below: The cool-house species, Brassia verrucosa, is a good beginner's orchid. Long sprays of fragrant flowers are produced in the early summer months.

(8-9in) across. The heavy, round lip is purple with a yellow patch inside the lobes.

First raised in 1941, this plant has been a very popular hybrid ever since. It has also produced some excellent offspring that continue the line of rich pink-purple colouring. It is typical of modern hybrids with three separate genera in its pedigree. These are *Brassavola, Laelia* and *Cattleya*. The qualities of all three have combined to give size and colour to the flower. These hybrids can be grown indoors provided they are given extremely good light.

In addition they require some rest after they have flowered in the winter, or until the new growth begins to show. During the rest the pseudobulbs should not be allowed to shrivel extensively.

Brassolaeliocattleya Crusader

☐ Intermediate: 13°C (55°F)
☐ Winter flowering
☐ Evergreen/some rest

This robust hybrid is the result of a cross between *Brassolaelio-cattleya* Queen Elizabeth and *Laeliocattleya* Trivanhoe, and requires intermediate temperature conditions. The large pink flowers, produced in winter, are 20-23cm

Below: Brassolaeliocattleya Crusader is a beautiful intermediate house hybrid. It produces large fragrant flowers in the spring or autumn that will last for three to four weeks.

Not only are bulbophyllums widely distributed throughout the subtropical and tropical areas of the world, but their vegetative growth habit and flower size and shape are also equally varied. Some flowers are so small, a magnifier is needed.

They comprise the largest genus in the orchid family, containing about 2000 species.

- ☐ Intermediate: 13°C (55°F)
- ☐ Spring flowering
- ☐ Evergreen/semi-rest

Bulbophyllum collettii

Coming from Burma, this is a plant for the intermediate house; it flowers during the spring. It has roundish, angular pseudobulbs spaced well apart on a creeping rhizome. The four to six flowers, produced on a flower spike that appears when the new growth is only partly completed, have lower sepals that hang down, as if joined, to a length of 13cm (5in). The top sepal and petals carry tufts of soft, fine hairs that flutter in even a slight air movement. The overall flower colour is maroon-red with yellow stripes.

This plant is not deeply rooted, and does best in shallow pots or on tree fern or cork bark. Good drainage is essential.

Left: Bulbophyllum collettii is an extraordinary species that can be grown in an intermediate greenhouse. It flowers in spring.

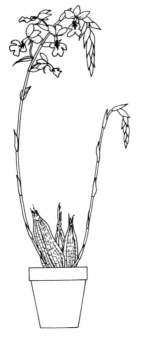

Calanthe vestita

warm-house conditions, it grows easily and is thus a good plant for beginners. Of the 150 species known, most are terrestrials; they come from a wide area including South Africa, Asia and Central America.

The flowers of *Calanthe vestita* range in colour from white to deep pink, the lip often being stronger in colour than the rest of the flower.

A warm greenhouse with good light suits this plant best. This deciduous species produces rather large, angular pseudobulbs with wide, ribbed leaves. During the growing season the plant should be liberally watered and fed until the leaves turn yellow and fall during the early winter months. At this stage watering should be gradually reduced. After flowering the pseudobulbs should be repotted in a well-drained compost with the addition of a little dried cow manure in the base.

☐ Warm: 18°C (65°F)
☐ Winter flowering
☐ Deciduous/dry rest

With tall, upright flower spikes and many long-lasting flowers, *Calanthe* is deservedly a special favourite with orchid growers. Given

Below: A very fine winter-flowering plant for the warm greenhouse, Calanthe vestita is a deciduous species which blooms while at rest.

Cattleya aurantiaca

This small bifoliate species comes from Guatemala and neighbouring countries. It has drooping clusters of red-orange flowers, 7.5-10cm (3-4in) across, produced in summer. The plant is peculiar in that it produces seedpods by self-pollination, which means that often the flowers do not open properly and the prettiness of the flowers is lost. Today plants are raised from selected nursery stock that produces fully opening flowers.

This species is one of the smallest growing and flowering varieties of *Cattleya* in cultivation. The plant will flower when only 15cm (6in) tall and is therefore easily accommodated in a small greenhouse or indoor growing case. Because of its diminutive pseudobulbs, *Cattleya aurantiaca* should not be allowed to remain in a dry state for any prolonged period. It is at its best when grown on into a large mature plant without being divided.

Above: Cattleya aurantiaca is one of the smallest of the cattleya species. This pretty plant flowers in summer and enjoys cool growth.

☐ Cool: 11°C (52°F)
☐ Summer flowering
☐ Evergreen/slight rest

Cattleya bowringiana

Below: The orchid Cattleya bowringiana grows best in the intermediate house. The large attractive flowers emerge in autumn.

This highly productive plant can produce as many as 20 rose-purple blooms, 7.5cm (3in) across, with a deep purple lip, marked with yellowish white in the throat. It requires more water than most to support the long pseudobulbs, which are slightly bulbous at the base. The flowers open during late autumn, and the plant benefits from a short mid-winter rest after flowering, during which time watering should be withheld.

This is an excellent plant for a beginner although it is now becoming increasingly difficult to obtain. The plant is slow growing from seed, and is not therefore readily available as nursery-raised stock. However, it can be grown and propagated with ease, so it is worth looking out for. Like all cattleyas it prefers a well-drained compost and is intolerant of soggy conditions.

This species originates from Guatemala and grows epiphytically in the wild. Some very interesting hybrids have been raised from it since its introduction in 1884.

☐ Intermediate: 11-13°C (52-55°F)
☐ Autumn flowering
☐ Evergreen/winter rest

Cattleya forbesii

Discovered in Brazil in 1823, this plant is a bifoliate of dainty growth, with pencil-thin pseudobulbs. Its yellow or tan-coloured flowers, produced in summer, are 7.5-10cm (3-4in) across, and have a tubular lip with side lobes of pale pink on the outside, and a deep yellow throat marked with wavy red lines.

This is an easy plant for the beginner and is also suitable for culture in an indoor growing case. It should not be overpotted, but kept in as small a pot as possible; unlike many cattleyas it rarely becomes top heavy. It should be grown in a position of good light all the year round and during the summer months can be lightly sprayed with water, taking care to avoid the flowers while in bloom. At one time this plant was considered a rather insignificant member of the genus, but today its smaller, pastel flowers are welcomed as charming and delicate.

This species has been little used for hybridizing. The plant can be propagated by careful division when large enough.

☐ Intermediate: 13°C (55°F)
☐ Late summer flowering
☐ Evergreen/semi-rest

Cymbidium Angelica 'Advent'
AM/RHS

This superb autumn to winter flowering yellow hybrid (*Cym. Lucy Moor* x *Cym. Lucense*) is fast becoming a very famous breeding plant and is being used by cymbidium hybridists throughout the world. Up to 14 large flowers, 13cm (5in) across, are carried on upright spikes. The petals and sepals are pale yellow and the cream-coloured lip is lightly spotted with dark red, the spotting becoming dense in the throat.

Cymbidium hybrids can become considerably large, and are best suited to a greenhouse where sufficient room can be given them. Overhead spraying is particularly beneficial during the summer growing season. If grown too warm without the cool night temperature recommended, the plants are unlikely to flower the following season. This is one of the earliest of the top class cymbidiums to bloom, and with careful selection of varieties the season can exceed six months. This very attractive cymbidium deserves a place in every collection.

Above: Cymbidium Angelica 'Advent' is cool-growing and an easy beginner's orchid. A good variety for autumn and winter flowers.

□ Cool: 10°C (50°F)
□ Autumn/winter flowering
□ Evergreen/no rest

are crimson tinged with white and the lip is a rich dark crimson, boldly edged with white.

A supporting cane will be required by most of these *Cymbidium* hybrids to prevent the heavy flower spikes snapping or buckling under their own weight as they develop. Though these flowers will last eight or ten weeks on the plant, it is advisable (particularly with young plants) to remove the spike after the last flower has been open for about ten days. This reduces the strain on the plant at a time when new growths are appearing. The cut spike of flowers will last just as long in water in a cool room indoors.

This is one of the easiest orchids to propagate. The old leafless pseudobulbs can be removed from the plant at repotting time and potted singly.

Cymbidium Ayres Rock 'Cooksbridge Velvet'

☐ Cool 10°C (50°F)
☐ Winter/spring flowering
☐ Evergreen/no rest

One of a new generation of cymbidiums in which the colour range has been extended even further towards the deeper pinks. The flowers, 11cm (4.25in) across,

Below: The fine, dark-flowered hybrid Cymbidium Ayres Rock 'Cooksbridge Velvet' blooms in spring. The flowers can last as long as 10 weeks.

Above: Cymbidium Fort George 'Lewes' is a cool-growing hybrid. The flowers emerge on its upright spikes in winter and spring.

flowers are up to 12cm (4.75in) in diameter. The bringing together of two of the most famous green-flowered parents (*Cym*. Baltic x *Cym*. York Meradith) has produced an excellent result.

To achieve regular flowering all cymbidiums should be repotted every other year, keeping them as large as can be managed. They can be fed throughout almost the whole year, reducing both feed and water to a minimum during the shortest days for three months of the year.

The blooms of cymbidiums are highly in demand as cut flowers and are certainly more popular with florists than any other orchid bloom. For this purpose they can be grown in large beds, where they grow exceedingly well, producing even more vigorous plants than those raised individually in pots in the accepted way.

Cymbidium Fort George 'Lewes'
AM/RHS

One of the finest free-flowering, green-coloured cymbidiums in the world, often giving two spikes per bulb with up to 14 flowers per spike on an upright stem. The

☐ Cool: 10°C (50°F)
☐ Winter/spring flowering
☐ Evergreen/no rest

Cymbidium Stonehaven 'Cooksbridge'

This second generation *Cym. pumilum* hybrid (*Cym.* Putana x *Cym.* Cariga) is a very good quality, medium-sized plant that produces strong spikes with up to 25 fine, 7cm (2.75in) flowers. Opening in autumn and early winter, the flowers are cream-coloured and the lip is pale yellow, edged with dark red. The plant is very free-flowering and easy to grow. Such plants are becoming increasingly popular as pot plants for the home.

While the flower spikes are developing, some support will be required. A thin bamboo cane should be inserted close to the spike and tied into position. The developing buds should not be supported until they are well developed, or the supporting ties must be adjusted almost daily as the spike grows. If the recommended night-time temperature cannot be kept down, the plant will be reluctant to bloom. During the summer such plants can be grown out of doors while temperatures permit.

- ☐ Cool: 10°C (50°F)
- ☐ Autumn/winter flowering
- ☐ Evergreen/no rest

and early spring. The flowers are bronze with contrasting deep crimson lips and are 2.5-4cm (1-1.5in) across.

An ideal beginner's plant for indoor or greenhouse culture. It should be kept watered throughout the year, never being allowed to dry out completely. During the spring, summer and autumn months the plant should be lightly fed. Cool night-time temperatures are important for successful flowering. Repotting will be necessary every other year. This should be done immediately after flowering and using a size larger pot. If there are too many leafless pseudobulbs, some should be removed to restore the balance of the plant. Water should be withheld for a few days after repotting is completed.

Cymbidium Touchstone 'Janis'

☐ Cool: 10°C (50°F)
☐ Winter/spring flowering
☐ Evergreen/no rest

This miniature variety is a fine example of *Cym. devonianum* breeding (*Cym. devonianum* x Mission Bay). The plants from this crossing are small and free growing, and produce beautiful arching sprays of flowers during the winter

Below: Cymbidium Touchstone 'Janis' is a beautiful miniature hybrid that carries semi-pendent spikes in the winter and spring. It is compact and cool-growing.

Dendrobium aureum

A widely distributed species found throughout India and in the Philippine Islands. The Indian variety is in general cultivation: the Philippine variety may be offered under the name of *D. heterocarpum*. The type produces stoutish bulbs of medium length and is deciduous in winter, when it needs a definite rest. Water should be discontinued when the leaves turn yellow and drop off naturally. A position of good light is essential during the winter to encourage flowering in the spring. The flowers appear during the early spring months, making it one of the first dendrobiums to flower. The blooms, up to 5cm (2in) across, are creamy-yellow with a buff brown lip covered in short hairs. They are pleasantly fragrant.

During the growing season keep a lookout for red spider mite, which can attack this plant. It is easily propagated from old canes cut into sections, or new plants can be raised from adventitious growths on old canes. Repot after flowering.

- ☐ Cool: 10°C (50°F)
- ☐ Early spring flowering
- ☐ Deciduous/dry winter rest

Above: Dendrobium densiflorum is one of the most beautiful of the spring-flowering species. Dense golden-yellow trusses are freely

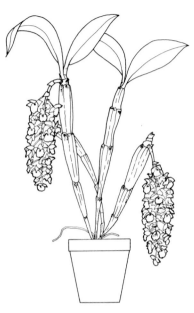

Dendrobium densiflorum

produced in the spring. The plant is cool-growing and keeps its leaves all winter. It is becoming rare in cultivation.

Once plentiful, this delightful species is becoming increasingly difficult to obtain. The flowers, up to 5cm (2in) across, are carried in large pendent trusses from nodes at the top half of the club-shaped bulbs. They develop at great speed during the spring months and last for up to ten days in perfection. Their colour is a brilliant golden yellow, the lip similarly coloured and very striking. The plant likes to be grown in the cool greenhouse with a decided rest in the winter.

The rest period should be commenced as soon as the season's canes have matured and produced new terminal leaf. The plant will flower from the older canes, which may or may not be in leaf. Full light during the autumn and winter is important for regular flowering. Keep the plant dry while in flower to extend flowering.

Not easy to propagate; grow on to a large plant and divide if required. Repot when new growth is seen. This species is evergreen and loses only a few leaves each year.

- ☐ Cool: 10°C (50°F)
- ☐ Spring flowering
- ☐ Evergreen/dry winter rest

Dendrobium nobile

Perhaps the most popular of all the cool-growing dendrobiums, this superb plant from India blooms during the spring. The flowers appear in ones and twos along the complete length of the previous year's bulbs, which are fairly tall and stoutish. The flowers, 5cm (2in) across, are rosy purple at the petal tips, shading to white towards the centre of the bloom. The lip carries a rich maroon blotch in the throat.

During the winter rest water should be withheld until the flower buds have clearly started their development in the spring. If watering is started too early embryo flower buds will develop into adventitious growths. Water the plants well all summer, and keep cool. Too high temperatures will restrict flowering.

Propagates easily from leafless canes, or new plants can be raised from adventitious growths. Do not overpot. If the plant becomes top heavy put the pot into a larger weighted container. Repot when new growth appears.

- ☐ Cool: 10°C (50°F)
- ☐ Spring flowering
- ☐ Semi-deciduous/dry rest

Above: Large flowered and highly fragrant, Dendrobium superbum is well suited for the warm greenhouse.

Below: A very popular and cool-growing species, Dendrobium nobile blooms in the spring. It flowers the length of the bulb.

Dendrobium superbum

One of the finest dendrobiums from the Philippine Islands, this is a deciduous species that produces extremely long canes. The fragrant flowers appear during the early summer, along the entire length of the previous year's canes; they are 5-6cm (2-2.4in) across, and a rich magenta-purple, the lip a deeper shade. There is also a variety *album*, which produces pure white flowers. Although rarer in cultivation it can sometimes be found. The very long canes make this species ideal for growing upside-down on a wooden raft.

This species will occasionally propagate from old canes, but it is best when grown into a large plant. Be wary of attack from red spider mite during the growing season. When the leaves turn yellow withhold water until flowering starts in the following spring. If grown in a pot, careful staking will be required. Remove old canes only when brown and shrivelled. Repot when the new growth is clearly seen.

- ☐ Warm: 16-18°C (60-65°F)
- ☐ Early summer flowering
- ☐ Deciduous/dry winter rest

Above: Epidendrum ibaguense can become very tall. It is a cool-growing, reed-type species that flowers at various times.

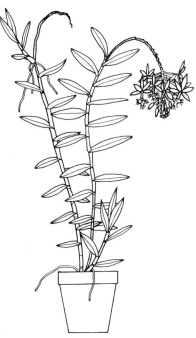

Epidendrum ibaguense

Often known as *E. radicans*, this is a reed-stem species. The stems vary from 60-150cm (2-5ft) in height according to environment and produce rounded leaves and many aerial roots over most of their length. The flowers (2.5cm; 1in) are orange-red or scarlet, the lip flat and very frilled. This is a plant for the cool greenhouse with good light. One successful specimen is known to have flowered continuously for four years.

The epidendrums are one of the largest genera: over 1000 species are known, coming mainly from Central and South America. So varied are the plants accepted within the genus, in vegetation and flower size and appearance, that some groups have been accorded a genus of their own. Those that remain within the genus are epiphytic.

Epidendrums seem to divide naturally into two categories: those with oval or rounded pseudobulbs, and those that produce reed-like stems.

- ☐ Cool: 9°C (48°F)
- ☐ Varied flowering season
- ☐ Evergreen/no rest

Epidendrum stamfordianum

This Central American species produces tall, club-shaped pseudobulbs that carry two or three thick leaves. The branching flower spike comes from the base of the plant, a unique feature among the epidendrums. The flower spike is many flowered; the fragrant blooms are yellow, spotted with red. The plant likes to be grown fairly warm, in a position of good light, and is therefore best suited to an intermediate greenhouse. It should be well watered during the summer growing season and allowed a complete winter's rest. The plant may be grown in a pot or on bark, where it will grow an extensive aerial root system. Propagation is best achieved by division of the main plant when it is large enough.

This large-growing plant is a good example of a bulb-type epidendrum as distinct from the reed type. It is also one of the most attractive epidendrums, although it is not frequently seen in collections.

□ Intermediate: 13°C (55°F)
□ Early summer flowering
□ Evergreen/dry rest

Above: The attractive fragrant flowers of Epidendrum stamfordianum grow on branching spikes from the base. The flowers bloom in summer and the plant thrives in the intermediate house.

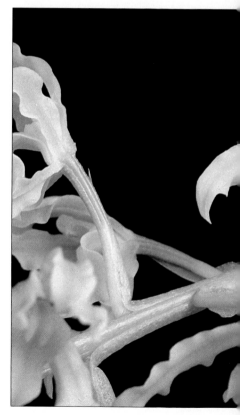

reason it is a good subject to grow on a raft or piece of cork bark. If grown in a pot, a coarse material, such as fir bark, should be used. As the plant grows upwards, away from the pot, the roots should be allowed to grow outside, where they should gain sufficient nourishment from the atmosphere. Spraying during the summer is helpful.

The plant produces pseudobulbs and leaves similar to those of odontoglossums, only paler in colour. The flowers are carried on arching sprays, up to 23cm (9in) long, and there are often two sprays to a pseudobulb. The sweetly scented, lime-green flowers, about 1.25cm (0.5in) across, are densely clustered on the spike and appear during the summer and autumn.

Gomeza crispa

A lthough there are about ten species of this epiphytic orchid available to growers, only one, *Gomeza crispa,* from Brazil is grown.

It is a plant for the cool house, requiring some protection from full light during the summer months. Free drainage for the root system is of great importance and for this

☐ Cool: 10°C (50°F)
☐ Summer/autumn flowering
☐ Evergreen/no rest

Below: Gomeza crispa is a small grower suitable for the cool house. Dainty lime-green sprays of flowers appear in the summer and autumn. This is an easy orchid for beginners.

appearance both plant and flower are similar to the cattleyas, with which many intergeneric hybrids have been made, it is a delightful genus in its own right, and is favoured by many growers. As with cattleyas, its flower spikes are produced from the apex of the pseudobulbs. The flower spike grows erect to 60cm (2ft) or more and produces two to five flowers, each about 10cm (4in) across. They are pale or deep rose-pink in colour, the lip being a darker hue than the other segments.

This is an excellent species for the beginner. It can be grown easily in a cool greenhouse or indoors, where it enjoys light conditions. If preferred, it can be grown on a block of wood or cork bark, when an extensive aerial root system will develop.

Propagation is a simple matter of separating the back bulbs and potting them up singly, when they will develop new growths.

Laelia anceps

S ome 75 species of *Laelia* have been recorded, almost all from Mexico and the northern parts of South America. Though in

☐ Cool: 10°C (50°F)
☐ Autumn flowering
☐ Evergreen/dry winter rest

Below: An extremely popular cool-house species, Laelia anceps is ideal for the novice. The flowers bloom from a tall stem in autumn. It also blooms well indoors.

Right: Lycaste aromatica is a deciduous cool house species that produces its single fragrant blooms in the spring. It requires a cool resting period.

on a stem about 15cm (6in) long. There may be as many as ten flowers to each pseudobulb.

The plant needs moisture and warmth when in full growth, but take care not to get water on the large, broad leaves, as they tend to develop brown spots if this occurs. Cooler and drier conditions are essential when the plant is at rest and in flower.

Propagation is by removal of the older pseudobulbs, which should not remain on the plant for too many years. It is better to restrict the size of the plant to five or six bulbs, provided they remain about the same size; should the bulbs become smaller, remove all but three or four.

Between 30 and 40 *Lycaste* species are known, including both terrestrial and epiphytic plants, most of which come from Central America. Many are also deciduous, losing their leaves during the winter.

Lycaste aromatica

As the name suggests, this species is heavily scented. The bright yellow flowers, 5cm (2in) across, often appear at the same time as the new growth, and are carried singly

- ☐ Cool/intermediate: 10-13°C (50-55°F)
- ☐ Winter/spring flowering
- ☐ Deciduous/dry winter rest

Lycaste deppei

Ⓞne of the most attractive of the lycastes, this plant produces fewer but larger, longer lasting flowers than *L. aromatica* – up to 11.5cm (4.5in) in diameter. The sepals are mid-green in colour spotted with reddish-brown, and the smaller petals are pure white. The lip is yellow in colour and also spotted with reddish-brown.

The plant has a fast growing season, when it should be given slightly higher temperatures combined with ample watering and feed. When repotting, a little old dried cow manure can be included in the compost. Repotting is best done annually; because of the extended dry rest period fresh compost is essential. The leaves, which can grow quite large, should be kept dry at all times; they are susceptible to water marks, which will show as ugly black or brown patches. While in growth, the plants will take up rather more room in the greenhouse. Because they require warmer growing conditions and cooler winter quarters with high light, they are not so easy to grow indoors.

- ☐ Cool/intermediate: 10-13°C (50-55°F)
- ☐ Winter/spring flowering
- ☐ Deciduous/dry winter rest

Below: A most attractive plant, Lycaste deppei produces long lasting flowers in the winter and spring months. It is best repotted annually.

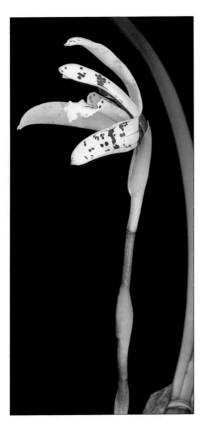

Maxillaria picta

This is one of the prettiest and most popular of the genus. The plant has roundish pseudobulbs topped by two long, narrow leaves. The 5cm (2in) flowers, produced prolifically on single stems, are yellow on the inside of the sepals and petals. On the outside are reddish-brown bars that show through to the inside. The lip is creamy white and slightly spotted in red. This lovely species flowers in profusion during the middle of the winter and has a pleasant, strong fragrance.

During the summer the plant should be kept moist and lightly fed, with a decided rest in good light after the season's growth is completed. The flowering stems appear at the same time as the new growths, the stems being rounded and fatter. Several new growths can be produced in a season, resulting in a good-sized plant within a few years. Propagation is by division of the plant when large enough. This pretty orchid can be grown in a cool greenhouse or indoors.

- ☐ Cool: 10°C (50°F)
- ☐ Winter flowering
- ☐ Evergreen/dry winter rest

Above: This species, Maxillaria picta, grows in the cool house and blooms during the winter. The single blooms are extremely pretty, fragrant and long lasting.

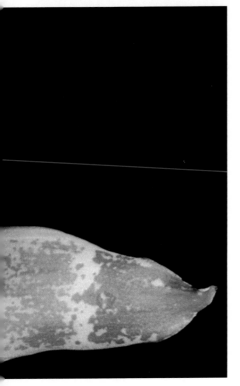

The plant has a very strong scent similar to that of coconut.

Because of its creeping habit it will quickly grow out of its pot and it is therefore more easily accommodated on a slab of wood. Grown vertically in this way, the plant quickly makes itself at home. It makes new roots sparingly and usually from the older bulbs around its base. The flowers, though not numerous, cluster around the bulbs on extremely short stems. Their bright colouring makes them eye-catching.

This is a plant that thrives in light conditions and dislikes too much moisture around its base. A well-drained compost is important if the plant is grown in a pot. During the summer it can be kept just moist by overhead spraying.

Maxillaria tenuifolia

☐ Cool: 10°C (50°F)
☐ Summer flowering
☐ Evergreen/semi-dry rest

I n this species a creeping rhizome, which grows almost vertically, produces small oval pseudobulbs at 2.5-5cm (1-2in) intervals. The flowers, 2.5cm (1in) across, are dark or bright red speckled with yellow.

Below: Maxillaria tenuifolia blooms in the summer, producing short-stemmed, strongly scented flowers. A small-growing species well suited for the cool house.

Above: The colours and markings of Odontocidium Tigersun 'Nutmeg' make this hybrid a unique specimen. Easy to grow in a cool house or indoors, it does not have a definite resting period.

Odontocidium Tigersun 'Nutmeg'

The introduction of *Oncidium* species into the breeding of odontoglossum hybrids has increased in popularity over the last few years and many hybrids are becoming available. Apart from giving different types of flowers and colours, most of the odontocidiums will stand more extreme conditions than the pure odontoglossums – which is of great importance to growers in warmer climates or where a mixed collection is cultivated. *Odontocidium* Tigersun is a cross between *Oncidium tigrinum* (a popular scented species from Mexico) and *Odontoglossum* Sunmar, and produces excellent bright yellow flowers, 9cm (3.5in) across, of good substance.

In common with other intergeneric odontoglossums, this hybrid does not have a definite resting period. It should be watered throughout the year, although less so during the winter. The only time this plant is not growing is while it is in flower, which can be six or eight weeks.

- ☐ Cool/intermediate: 10-13°C (50-55°F)
- ☐ Varied flowering season
- ☐ Evergreen/no rest

*Right: The popular species
Odontoglossum grande flourishes in
a cool environment. The very showy,
clown-like flowers appear during the
autumn months. After flowering,
give the plant a winter rest.*

*Below: The Odontoglossum
bictoniense from Guatemala
produces tall, upright spikes. This
species is cool-growing and flowers
in late summer.*

Odontoglossum bictoniense

This is one of the easiest and most popular species, and an ideal plant for beginners. Native to Guatemala, it is a very vigorous grower and will quickly grow into a specimen plant. Erect flower spikes appear at the end of the summer, growing quickly in warm weather to reach heights up to 122cm (48in) and bearing 20 long-lasting flowers on each spike. The flowers open in succession so that there are usually eight or nine out at once over a period of several weeks. The flowers are about 3-4cm (1.25-1.5in) across, yellowy green with brown spots and a striking white or pink lip.

Odontoglossum bictoniense, which can be grown successfully as a houseplant, requires cool conditions with medium shade and does not need resting in winter, though water should be reduced when flowering has finished, until new growth appears in the spring.

This species is very variable. The plant is easily propagated from the leafless pseudobulbs.

□ Cool: 10°C (50°F)
□ Summer flowering
□ Evergreen/semi-rest

Odontoglossum grande

K nown widely as the 'clown orchid' due to the clown-like figure represented by the column in the centre of the flower, this is certainly one of the most widely grown in this genus, and popular as a houseplant. The flowers are very large, up to 15cm (6in) across, yellow with bright chestnut-brown markings.

It has hard dark leaves and very tough pseudobulbs, and needs a decided rest during the winter months. During the growing season it needs plenty of moisture at the roots but excessive atmospheric moisture can result in unsightly black spotting on the foliage. As the new growth starts to make a pseudobulb towards the end of the summer the flower spike develops, and the flowers usually open in autumn. Once flowering is finished and the pseudobulbs have fully matured, watering should be withheld until spring, when the new growth appears. The plants need light shade and should be grown in a medium-grade bark compost. They should receive full light in winter.

□ Cool: 10°C (50°F)
□ Autumn flowering
□ Evergreen/dry winter rest

Odontoglossum pulchellum

Above: Odontoglossum pulchellum is a cool-house species that flowers in spring. Sprays of small, waxy, fragrant flowers bloom abundantly from the delicate spikes.

An extremely popular and vigorous Guatemalan species. The waxy, white flowers, though small – 1-2cm (0.4-0.8in) across – bloom in masses and have a lovely scent, which explains why it is known as the 'lily of the valley orchid'. It flowers in spring and produces more than one shoot from each pseudobulb, making it ideal for growing into a specimen. The plants are thin-rooted and need cool conditions, a fine-grade bark mix, and medium shade in the summer.

If left unsupported the slender flower spikes will often assume a pendent position by the time they are in bloom. If an upright position is preferred, the spikes should be lightly tied to thin supporting canes, when the flowers will stand well clear of the foliage. This is an unusual species, which alone among the cultivated odontoglossums carries its flowers with the lip uppermost.

Within the genus, it has not contributed to any hybridization.

It can be easily propagated by the removal of back bulbs.

- □ Cool: 10°C (50°F)
- □ Spring flowering
- □ Evergreen/slight rest

A typical variety produces star-shaped flowers in winter, about 3-5cm (1.25-2in) across, white with brown markings; rarer varieties are flushed with pink, or deep pink. Probably the most popular is the Majus variety, which has a much larger flower up to 7.5cm (3in) across. However, this sought after variety is seldom seen today; the smaller forms are usually grown.

Because of their small size, the pseudobulbs should not be allowed to shrivel at any time. During the winter, when the plant is inactive for a short period, watering should be lessened slightly.

Odontoglossum rossii

From Guatemala and Mexico, this is one of the most delightful of the miniature odontoglossums. The plants are thin-rooted and flourish in cool conditions and a fine bark mix or sphagnum moss that will keep them moist at all times. Medium shade is required during the summer.

☐ Cool: 10°C (50°F)
☐ Winter flowering
☐ Evergreen/no rest

Below: Odontoglossum rossii is a delightful miniature species for the cool house. It produces lovely long-lasting flowers in winter.

Oncidium ornithorhynchum

An extremely showy species from Mexico and Guatemala, this plant has a compact habit and light green pseudobulbs each topped with several thin leaves. The short, slender and arching flower spikes are produced very freely in the autumn and carry the individual flowers on side branches. These are about 2cm (0.8in) long, the sepals and petals curled and twisted. The colour is a soft rose-lilac with a yellow crest on the lip. They are long-lasting and beautifully fragrant. It is not unusual for two or three flower spikes to be produced by one bulb.

Propagation is by division and removal of back bulbs, although the plant is at its best when grown on into a specimen. A very fine rooting system is produced, indicating that a well-drained compost is important. The plant dislikes cold and damp and should therefore not be sprayed overhead or kept too wet at any time. Otherwise, normal cool house conditions will suit it. It is a delightful beginner's orchid of great charm that will do equally well indoors.

- ☐ Cool: 10°C (50°F)
- ☐ Autumn flowering
- ☐ Evergreen/semi-rest

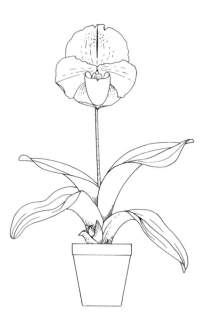

Paphiopedilum Honey Gorse 'Sunshine'
AM/RHS

The first plant to combine the characteristics of the green and the yellow paphiopedilum groups, the 10cm (4in) flowers of this hybrid are dark yellow-green. Deeper emerald green hybrids are now being bred, but this plant will take

Above: The pretty, miniature Oncidium ornithorhynchum is well suited for the cool house. It produces fragrant sprays of flowers on slender drooping spikes.

Left: Paphiopedilum Honey Gorse 'Sunshine' is for the intermediate house. This winter flowering hybrid produces a single, large flower per stem.

some beating for its heavy texture – a feature usually lacking in the green colour group.

The plant contrasts beautifully with the heavier coloured and spotted flowers in the other colour ranges. It offers the grower a clear, fresh alternative to enhance any collection.

The plant should be repotted annually to ensure fresh, free-draining compost while keeping the pot size as small as possible. An intermediate greenhouse will suit this hybrid type best, where shady conditions should prevail. These hybrids are usually slower growing than many of the species and therefore splitting is not normally recommended unless or until the plant has several large growths.

- ☐ Intermediate: 13°C (55°F)
- ☐ Winter flowering
- ☐ Evergreen/no rest

Below: The graceful flower of Paphiopedilum Maudiae is carried on a slender stem at various times of the year. Grows well in intermediate house conditions.

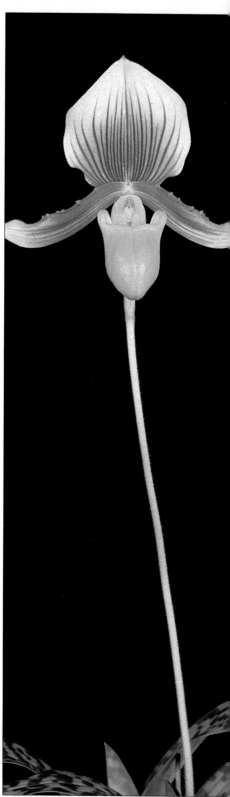

Paphiopedilum Maudiae

This is probably the most consistently popular *Paphiopedilum* hybrid in the world. The plant has the grace and beauty found among a few of the species, which have been overshadowed by the heavier, rounded type of hybrids. This hybrid results from a cross of *Paph. callosum* x *Paph. lawrenceanum*, using two green varieties.

The plant is a strong, vigorous grower than can be continually divided without harm to produce further plants. The foliage is beautifully mottled in light and dark green, the leaves are short and rounded. The tall, slender stem carries a single large bloom, distinctively marked in white and deep apple green. Its coloured variety, *Paph.* Maudiae 'Coloratum', shows the same markings on a rich purple ground.

Its ease of culture and long-lasting, long-stemmed blooms, which can be produced twice in one year, have made this hybrid popular for the cut flower trade.

☐ Intermediate: 13°C (55°F)
☐ Varied flowering season
☐ Evergreen/no rest

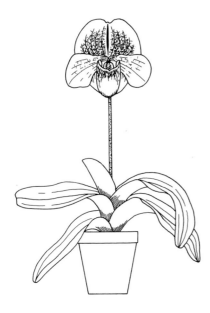

combination of soft rose-red shaded with green, open in the winter.

The plant should be grown in the intermediate greenhouse, under warm and shady conditions with an even moisture. Annual repotting is recommended to maintain the compost in a fresh and open condition and thus ensure a steady rate of growth. When in bloom, these heavy flowers will need the support of a thin bamboo cane and green string tie, or a thin wire stake. The blooms will last for up to ten weeks on the plant, after which the stem should be cut and the plant encouraged to make its new growth for the following season.

This plant can be recommended for beginners to orchid growing provided a warm and shady position is available for it to thrive.

Paphiopedilum Royale 'Downland'
AM/RHS & GMM

☐ Intermediate: 13°C (55°F)
☐ Winter flowering
☐ Evergreen/no rest

This hybrid is a seedling from the illustrious *P.* Paeony 'Regency' (AM/RHS) line, and has very large flowers, 15cm (6in) across, borne on long flower spikes. The flowers, which are an interesting colour

Below: Paphiopedilum Royale 'Downland' is an excellent red-flowered variety for the intermediate house. The single blooms are very long lasting during the winter months of the year.

Paphiopedilum venustum

The leaves of this species are heavily marbled with grey and green. One or, occasionally, two flowers, 7.5cm (3in) across, are borne on a 15-23cm (6-9in) stem. The petals and lip are basically yellow-green, tinged with rose-red, and the petals are slightly hairy. The dorsal sepal is white, strongly striped with green. The plant blooms in early spring.

This is an excellent choice for the intermediate greenhouse. The neat plant is attractive in and out of flower. The delightful flowers are showy and long-lasting. The species comes from the Himalayas and should be given shady conditions with a good fresh atmosphere. Regular repotting will ensure that the compost remains fresh and free-draining. This species, though still reasonably plentiful, has not been used in breeding new hybrids as extensively as a number of other paphiopedilums, and its influence is not noticeable in most of today's modern hybrids. An easy plant to grow and flower.

Above: Paphiopedilum venustum is a compact-growing species for the intermediate house. It flowers during the spring and will thrive in shady and airy conditions.

☐ Intermediate: 13°C (55°F)
☐ Spring flowering
☐ Evergreen/no rest

Phalaenopsis Hennessy

Below: Phalaenopsis Hennessy is ideal for a warm greenhouse when its flowers can be produced at various times of the year. This variety is known as 'candy striped'.

This hybrid is an example of a peppermint-striped phalaenopsis. The plant is very free-flowering, blooming throughout the year, and the branched spikes may bear up to 30 flowers at a time. The individual flowers are 9-12cm (3.5-4.75in) across, white to light pink in basic colour, with red or pink stripes or, in some forms, spots. The lip varies in colour from deep rosy pink to orange.

This hybrid type is of fairly recent breeding, and the plants are in limited supply. From a particular cross, only a percentage of the seedlings will carry the elusive candy-striped markings that are highly valued to increase the variety within the genus. *Phalaenopsis* flowers are highly susceptible to damp conditions, when premature spotting of the flowers will occur. A movement of air from an electric fan combined with a drier atmosphere while the plants are in bloom will help to prevent this common problem. The plants will also suffer if given poor light during the winter.

□ Warm: 18-21°C (65-70°F)
□ Varied flowering season
□ Evergreen/no rest

Phalaenopsis Temple Cloud

Resulting from the crossing of two outstanding hybrids, *P.* Opaline and *P.* Keith Shaffer, this hybrid took on the finer points of both parents, producing pure white 11.5cm (4.5in) round blooms of heavy texture, and in turn proved to be a very successful parent. It can be in flower at any season.

Like all the other modern *Phalaenopsis* hybrids it is not difficult to grow and can be in bloom for months at a time provided it is given plenty of warmth. This important factor makes it ideal for growing in an indoor case, where the high temperatures required can be more easily achieved. It is a shade-loving or low light plant, which enables it to be successfully grown and flowered in artificial light conditions. The plant should be grown in as small a pot as possible, in a free-draining bark compost. It should be fed at every third watering for most of the year, and never be allowed to dry out completely.

The flowers can be cut and used for flower arrangements.

□ Warm: 18°C (65°F)
□ Varied flowering season
□ Evergreen/no rest

Above right: Phalaenopsis Temple Cloud is a pure white hybrid for the warm house. It has varied flowering times.

Pleione formosana

U ntil recently orchid growers had not taken this genus seriously, unlike the alpine growers, who cultivate pleiones with great success. The 20 known species are found growing close to the snowline of the Himalayas, and also in parts of China and Formosa. The Himalayan species are probably better suited to the conditions of an alpine house, but others do well in the cool section of an orchid house.

The plant consists of a single, squat, roundish pseudobulb, which lasts for only one year. New growth springs from the base of the pseudobulb, and in its early stages produces a flower spike from its centre. This spike bears one or two flowers, up to 10cm (4in) across. The common species has flowers ranging from pure white to pale pinky-mauve. In all variations the broad lip is frilled, and in the coloured forms it is spotted with ginger or brick red.

In the early spring the plants should be taken from their pot, and reset about half-buried in a fine but well-draining compost.

☐ Very cool: 4.5°C (40°F)
☐ Spring flowering
☐ Evergreen/dry rest

Below: Pleione formosana is a relatively easy and reliable orchid. It will grow cool in an alpine house, flowering in spring. It is called 'oriental splendour'.

Polystachya pubescens

Above: Polystachya pubescens is an unusual species for the intermediate house. It comes from tropical Africa, is small-growing and blooms at various times.

The majority of the 150 known species of *Polystachya* come from tropical Africa. Though the flowers are generally small, the plants flower freely under cultivation.

These plants are subjects for the intermediate house. Being epiphytic, they require a well-drained compost, but plenty of moisture at the root while the plant is in active growth. Moderate protection from the full sun is also required. Polystachyas undoubtedly do best when left undisturbed for several years.

A notable feature is that the flowers appear upside-down on the spike, the lip being uppermost with the two sepals, normally at the base of the flower, forming a hood.

This species produces narrow, tapering pseudobulbs, which grow to a height of 5cm (2in) and have two or three short leaves. The flower spike comes from the apex of the pseudobulb and carries six to 12 bright yellow flowers, each up to 1.5cm (0.6in) across, the upper sepals and lip of which are marked delicately with red lines.

- □ Intermediate: 13°C (55°F)
- □ Varied flowering season
- □ Evergreen/no rest

Potinara Sunrise

With colourful magenta flowers and slightly darker lips, this hybrid is the result of a quadrigeneric cross (*Brassavola* x *Cattleya* x *Laelia* x *Sophronitis*). The flowers, which open in the autumn, are 13-15cm (5-6in) across and very showy.

Generally, the flowers of potinaras are of a slightly heavier texture, with better lasting qualities. The flowers will become prematurely spotted, however, in over-moist conditions. As with all cattleya hybrids, it is advisable to keep the plants and their surroundings on the dry side while the plants are flowering.

Repotting may be carried out after flowering in the autumn or later in the spring. The aim should be to catch the new growths when they

are about 2.5cm (1in) long, just before the new roots appear. All intergeneric cattleyas do well when grown in good light and when given a rest after flowering until the new growth starts.

During the summer these plants can be lightly sprayed overhead, but the foliage should be dry well before nightfall.

- [ ] Intermediate: 13°C (55°F)
- [ ] Autumn flowering
- [ ] Evergreen/some rest

Below: The Potinara Sunrise is a lovely cattleya-type hybrid for autumn flowering in the intermediate house. It is best to keep the compost relatively dry, even during flowering.

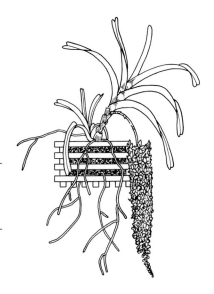

Rhynchostylis retusa

Four species make up this well-known and popular epiphytic genus, and all are seen in present-day collections.

Their natural habitat is Malaysia and Indonesia and, consequently, they enjoy reasonably warm conditions, similar to those of the strap-leaf vandas, which they resemble vegetatively. Because the flowers grow densely in cylindrical fashion on a pendent raceme or spike, they are commonly known as 'foxtail orchids', although this name is also given to other orchids that produce their flowers in similar fashion (eg *Aerides fieldingii*).

This species produces a plant up to 60cm (2ft) in height with a pendulous spike of 38-50cm (15-20in) which carries many thick, waxy and highly fragrant flowers, each up to 2cm (0.8in) in diameter. These are basically white but may be lightly or heavily spotted with magenta-purple. The hook-shaped lip is solid magenta. The flowers appear from winter to spring and last for only two or three weeks, but if well grown the plant will flower more often. (See illustration on page 94.)

- [ ] Intermediate: 13°C (55°F)
- [ ] Winter/spring flowering
- [ ] Evergreen/no rest

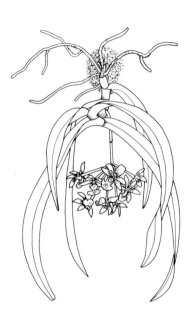

Saccolabium acutifolium

This species belongs to a small epiphytic group of about 20 species. It originates from India and is now more correctly *Gastrochilus acutifolius*, although the older name persists in horticulture. The plant produces upward growing (monopodial) stems from which grow the narrow, pointed leaves. The fragrant flowers come from between the leaves and are carried on a short, pendent stem in the form of a rosette. These are highly variable and can be pure yellow-green, shaded with brown to an almost solid red colouring. The lip is of curious shape, basically white, occasionally spotted in red with a central yellow stain, and frilled around the edge. It is the shape of the lip that gives the genus *Gastrochilus* its name: *gaster* (belly) and *cheilos* (lip).

The plant will grow happily on a piece of bark in a pendent position, when it will produce a number of dangling aerial roots. It should be kept permanently moist and prefers to be grown in fairly heavy shade. During the summer months it can be sprayed generously.

☐ Intermediate: 13°C (55°F)
☐ Autumn flowering
☐ Evergreen/no rest

Left: Native to tropical America, Stanhopea tigrina has magnificent but short-lived summer flowers. It is a highly fragrant species which grows well in a basket.

Above: Originating from India, Saccolabium acutifolium is an autumn flowering species that will grow particularly well mounted on a piece of bark.

Stanhopea tigrina

A bout 25 species of this fascinating genus have been described, although some may be variants rather than species. They are particularly remarkable for both their growth habit and their unusual flower shape. All are epiphytic and come from tropical America.

The flowering habit of stanhopeas is unusual in that the flower spike, which develops from the base of the pseudobulb, grows directly downwards through the compost to flower beneath the plant. For this reason, these orchids must be grown in wire or wooden-slatted baskets. Unfortunately, these highly fragrant flowers last for only about three days; nevertheless, the plants are of enormous interest and worthy of a place in any mixed collection of orchids.

The flowers of this species are over 10cm (4in) across. The basic colour is ivory or pale yellow, and the sepals and petals are heavily blotched with maroon-purple. It is a most striking species and very fragrant. A large plant will bloom very freely in succession.

□ Cool/intermediate:
   10-13°C (50-55°F)
□ Summer flowering
□ Evergreen/dry rest

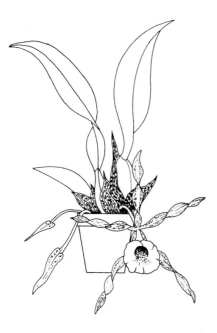

Trichopilia tortilis

About 30 species of *Trichopilia* are known, although only a few of these are available to growers today. Despite this, they remain very popular, partly because they are not difficult to cultivate and also because of their very showy flowers, which are large in comparison with the size of the plant. The plants are epiphytic and are found mainly in South America.

The plants, which never grow very tall, develop flattened pseudobulbs that may be rounded or elongated, and a solitary leathery leaf. Intermediate house conditions suit them well, with good shade during the summer months. The plants benefit from generous moisture at the root in full growth. After flowering, these orchids should be

allowed a period of semi-rest.

This plant carries a single flower, up to 13cm (5in) across, on a pendent spike. The sepals and petals, which are narrow and twisted throughout their length, are brown, bordered by a narrow yellow-green band; the trumpet-shaped lip is white with some rose-red spotting.

- ☐ Cool/intermediate:
  10-13°C (50-55°F)
- ☐ Summer flowering
- ☐ Evergreen/semi-rest

Below: Trichopilia tortilis is a summer-flowering species suited for the cool or intermediate greenhouse. After flowering, allow the plant to rest.

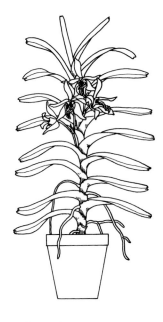

Vanda cristata

This small orchid, which grows only to about 25cm (10in), is a good subject for indoor growing. It is native to high-altitude areas of Nepal and Bhutan. The leaves are 15cm (6in) long and the flowers waxy and fragrant, about 5cm (2in) across. The sepals and petals are mostly yellow-green, and the entire flower is marked with blood-red longitudinal stripes and spots. Blooming from early spring until mid-summer, this is a fine orchid for those with limited space.

This species is one of the few vandas suitable for beginners. It flowers very freely on a modestly sized plant and the flowers last for many weeks. Regular spraying of the whole plant, except when in bloom, will encourage the growth of fat, aerial roots, which grow at right angles from the stem. When the green tips of the roots become concealed by a white covering the plant is at rest and should be kept semi-dry.

This plants enjoys a position of good light in the cool or intermediate greenhouse.

- ☐ Cool/intermediate:
  10-13°C (50-55°F)
- ☐ Spring/summer flowering
- ☐ Evergreen/semi-rest

Moderately Easy to Grow

As far as orchids are concerned, the plants featured in this section are moderately easy to grow, although they are still more difficult than most houseplants because of the space and facilities required to look after them while they are not flowering.

During the period when these orchids are not in bloom they need careful treatment in order to keep them healthy. With some of them, such as *Laelia cinnabarina*, low temperatures and damp can cause damage. Alternatively, if kept too dry for any length of time, the slender pseudobulbs will shrivel and die.

The specific requirements during the non-flowering period have been given for each species in this section, as well as information on the plants' general care throughout the year.

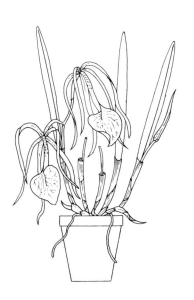

Brassavola nodosa

Chysis bractescens

Brassavolas are very popular with amateur growers, partly because they are easy to cultivate and also for the strange shapes of some of the flowers. The 15 species known are either epiphytic or lithophytic and come from Central and South America.

In this species the pseudobulbs and leaves are very slender and appear as one, both being cylindrical in shape. The plants are best grown on tree-fern fibre, with just a little compost, and suspended from the greenhouse roof. Brassavolas object to excessive moisture and should be kept quite dry during their lengthy period of rest. They do well in the conditions suitable for cattleyas.

Brassavola nodosa is very fragrant, especially in the cool of the evening or at night. It can be found in flower at any time of the year. The flowers, often four to five on a stem, are creamy-green and up to 7.5cm (3in) across when fully open. The lip is broad, and white with a few purple spots in the throat.

- ☐ Intermediate: 13°C (55°F)
- ☐ Variable flowering season
- ☐ Evergreen/dry rest

Left: Chysis bractescens is a summer flowering orchid that bears large white flowers on a single short stem.

The flowers of this species, up to 7.5cm (3in) in diameter, grow rather close together on a single but comparatively short stem produced from new growth. They are white turning to cream with age; the lip is white on the outer surface and tinged with yellow inside.

The six species of *Chysis* recorded, which come mainly from Mexico, are all epiphytic and semi-deciduous under cultivation. When in growth the plants require a liberal supply of heat and moisture; when they have shed their leaves they should be transferred to the cool house for a period of rest. During this time they should be kept much drier at the root until growth restarts in the spring.

Growth and form are similar in all the species. A few, often large, leaves grow from the upper half of the spindle-shaped pseudobulbs, which may be up to 46cm (18in) long. These either grow horizontally or hang down, so that the plants are best grown in baskets.

Repot every other year using a well-draining compost.

- ☐ Cool/Intermediate: 10-13°C (50-55°F)
- ☐ Early summer flowering
- ☐ Semi-deciduous/dry rest

Dendrobium Gatton Sunray

FCC/RHS

A magnificent hybrid, this is the largest of the cultivated dendrobiums, and requires plenty of growing space. It is an extremely robust plant, the canes growing to a height of 2m (6.5ft) or more. The extremely large and showy flowers, which appear in trusses during the early summer, are more than 10cm (4in) across and last in perfection for about ten days. A large plant will produce numerous trusses, each carrying several flowers. This will extend the flowering period, as not all the trusses come into flower at the same time.

The plant succeeds best in an intermediate greenhouse where it can be given good light and a decided rest during the winter months.

This plant is quite rare in cultivation and may take some finding. In view of its large size it should not be attempted where adequate space and light cannot be given. The propagation of this hybrid is very slow. Repot this plant every other year in the spring when the new growth is seen.

☐ Intermediate: 13°C (55°F)
☐ Summer flowering
☐ Evergreen/dry winter rest

Below left: Dendrobium Gatton Sunray is a massive grower that needs plenty of room in the intermediate greenhouse. Blooms are produced during the summer.

Above: An unusual hybrid for the intermediate house, Dendrobium Tangerine 'Tillgates' requires full light throughout the year. It is best grown in a greenhouse.

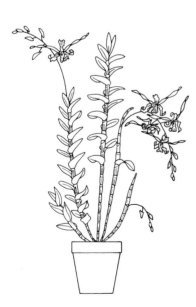

Dendrobium Tangerine 'Tillgates'

AM/RHS

Rather different from the 'traditional' cultivated dendrobium, this outstanding hybrid was raised from a little known but beautiful species, *D. strebloceras*, which comes from western New Guinea. Its name means 'crumpled horn' and refers to the long twisting petals. In the hybrid these petals stand erect, closely resembling the horns of an antelope. The plant is more colourful than its parent species, the 7.5cm (3in) flowers having bright orange petals and mustard yellow sepals and lip. Although the plant is little grown outside the tropics, its unusual and delightful flowers make it a desirable addition to any collection. A subject for the intermediate greenhouse, it would not do well as a houseplant, as it requires full light throughout the year.

The plant is of neat habit, producing elegant canes that are leafed at the top. Flowering is from the top of the canes. It does not propagate readily and should not be hastily divided.

☐ Intermediate: 13°C (55°F)
☐ Spring/summer flowering
☐ Semi-deciduous/semi-rest

Doritis pulcherrima

A native species of Southeast Asia, the attractive *Doritis pulcherrima* is much prized in modern collections and grows well in warm house conditions suitable for *Phalaenopsis*.

In plant habit and appearance it is much like *Phalaenopsis*, but is inclined to grow taller. It has three to four pairs of stiff grey-green leaves, spotted with dark purple on the upper surface.

The flower spikes are held upright and grow to a height of 60cm (24in) or more, producing ten to 25 flowers which open, a few at a time, on the upper half of the spike. Flowers appear at any season and often more than once in the same year. As individual flowers last for many weeks, a single spike can bloom for four or five months. The flowers vary widely in size (2-4cm; 0.75-1.5in) and colour; the sepals and petals range from pale rose-purple to deep magenta, with parts of the lip often of a deeper hue.

Doritis pulcherrima has been used extensively in hybridization, particularly with *Phalaenopsis*.

□ Warm: 18°C (65°F)
□ Varied flowering season
□ Evergreen/no rest

Below: Doritis pulcherrima is an attractive warm-house species with tall, upright spikes. The flowers appear at any season, and often twice a year. Treat as Phalaenopsis for successful cultivation.

Encyclia mariae

This stunning species bears one to five flowers on a thin, upright stem, each flower being about 5cm (2in) wide; the sepals and petals are lime green and the very broad lip, which is often the widest part of the flower, is pure white. *Encyclia mariae* is considered to be one of the loveliest of all the summer-flowering orchids.

Above: Large, showy flowers bloom from the small plant Encyclia mariae. This species is cool-growing and blooms in summer.

The flowers are extremely large for the size of the plant, and last well. The plant should not be heavily watered at any time and is intolerant of soggy conditions. Allow the plant to rest while not in active growth, and keep in a fairly shady aspect. Propagation from the oldest pseudobulbs is slow; it is better to leave them on the plant provided it is healthy. The plant should not be sprayed, as the leaves are susceptible to water marks.

This plant can also be grown on a piece of bark, where it should be allowed to remain undisturbed for a number of years. If too many leafless bulbs build up, these should be removed very carefully without disturbing the plant.

- ☐ Cool: 9°C (48°F)
- ☐ Summer flowering
- ☐ Semi-deciduous/dry rest

Grammangis ellisii

This species is a member of a small genus of remarkably handsome epiphytic orchids of which five species are known. It is a large robust plant that requires plenty of room in which to grow. The pseudobulbs are tall, spindle-shaped and four-sided, which is an unusual feature. Several long, leathery leaves are set towards the top half of the bulb. The flower spikes emerge from the half-completed new growth during the summer. These are naturally arching and many flowered. The slightly fragrant flowers are 9cm (3.5in) across and similar in shape to a *Lycaste* flower. The prominent sepals are basically yellow, this colour partially obscured by dense, reddish brown bars. The petals and lips are smaller.

The plant is suitable for a warm greenhouse and while growing should be watered and fed liberally. During the winter less water but extra light should be given. The plants do not like disturbance and should only be repotted when absolutely necessary. The plant is a native of Madagascar.

☐ Warm: 18°C (65°F)
☐ Summer flowering
☐ Evergreen/semi-rest

Laelia cinnabarina

This plant comes from Brazil and belongs to a group of brilliantly coloured species that are smaller in the size of their plants and flowers than the majority of laelias. This species has thin pseudobulbs, which are darker in colour than most, as is the leaf. Five to 12 star-shaped, orange-red flowers, each about 5cm (2in) across, are produced on a 23cm (9in) spike during the winter and spring. Due to importing restrictions this species is not now often seen in cultivation.

It likes intermediate conditions and is intolerant of cold and damp. The slender pseudobulbs will quickly shrivel if the plant is allowed to remain in a dry state for any length of time. It should be only semi-rested in winter, with sufficient water to ensure that the bulbs remain plump. The plant should be kept in as small a pot as possible and grown on into a good-sized plant. Propagation is by division when the plant is large enough.

This particular species has been used to some extent in interbreeding orchids, in order to increase colour in the hybrids.

☐ Intermediate: 13°C (55°F)
☐ Winter/spring flowering
☐ Evergreen/semi-dry rest

Above: Laelia cinnabarina is a neat-growing, intermediate-house species that produces colourful heads of flowers in winter and spring.

Laeliocattleya Chitchat 'Tangerine'

A summer-flowering hybrid bred from a cross between *C. aurantiaca* and *Laelia* Coronet. The plant, which has clusters of delicate yellow-orange flowers 5cm (2in) across, has slender pseudobulbs and should be grown in the intermediate section of the greenhouse.

This hybrid illustrates the diversity that can be found among the bigeneric cattleya hybrids. Here we see the less flamboyant flower with simpler lines, but with the superb colouring unique to the type. Also, having one species parent, the plant shows close resemblance to that species.

This plant grows in the same conditions as other cattleya intergeneric hybrids, but will usually have a shorter resting period. The pseudobulbs are more slender and will therefore shrivel more easily if water is withheld for long periods. Light overhead spraying is an advantage during the summer.

Repotting should be carried out in the spring unless the plant is in bud, in which case it should be repotted in the autumn.

- □ Intermediate: 13°C (55°F)
- □ Summer flowering
- □ Evergreen/some rest

Masdevallia coccinea

M asdevallia is one of the most fascinating orchid genera, as remarkable for the uniformity of its vegetation as for the diversity of form and colour of its flowers. Three hundred species are recorded, growing mainly in the higher-altitude areas of Mexico, Brazil and Colombia. The structure of the flowers is in contrast to that of many orchids, as the sepals are very large in comparison with the other parts of the flower.

This species produces leaves that are 30cm (12in) in length, and flower spikes which are often much taller. These bear a single flower of 7.5-10cm (3-4in), with sepals that taper sharply towards the tips. The range of colour varies from lilac to deep crimson.

Because of the high-altitude conditions of its natural habitat, the cool house with plenty of shade and fresh air during the summer months provides the ideal environment. Masdevallias do not produce pseudobulbs – the thick leaves spring directly from a creeping rhizome – so the plants should never be allowed to become dry.

- ☐ Cool: 10°C (50°F)
- ☐ Winter/spring flowering
- ☐ Evergreen/no rest

Opposite top: The very striking and unusual hybrid Laeliocattleya Chitchat 'Tangerine' is suitable for the intermediate house. It flowers in the summer months.

Above: Masdevallia coccinea is a very attractive species for the cool house. The single flowers are carried on a tall, slender stem during the winter and spring.

Masdevallia tovarensis

A beautiful species from Colombia that produces the typical neat growth of the genus. The leaves are glossy, dark green and grow from the base of the plant from a connecting rhizome. The flowering stems come from the base of the leaves and carry two to four flowers clear of the foliage. When the flowers have died, the stem remains green and blooms again the following year, an unusual feature for an orchid. The attractive flowers are a soft powdery white and are largely composed of the three sepals, which are elongated and end with a short tail.

Odontoglossum-type culture suits these orchids well. They should be grown in cool, airy conditions and kept just moist at all times. The plants will quickly deteriorate if allowed to get too wet or too cold at any time. A well-drained compost and regular repotting are essential. Several new growths will be produced each growing season, enabling a large plant to be built up in a comparatively short time. Propagation is by division when the plant is large enough.

- ☐ Cool: 10°C (50°F)
- ☐ Autumn flowering
- ☐ Evergreen/no rest

Miltonia clowesii

This is a Brazilian plant, with pseudobulbs, whose leaves reach a height of about 50cm (20in). The flower spike, which may be up to 60cm (2ft) in length, grows from the base of the pseudobulb and bears six to ten flowers, each about 6.5cm (2.5in) across. The sepals and petals are of equal size, reddish-brown and barred with yellow. The lip, in direct contrast, is white with a pinky-mauve blotch on its upper part.

Twenty species of this deservedly popular genus have been recorded. The majority are very sweet-scented and flower throughout the year, often more than once. They divide roughly into two natural groups. In the first group are plants from Brazil, which produce yellowish-green foliage and flattened pseudobulbs, well spaced on a creeping rhizome. These orchids require intermediate conditions and more light than plants in the second group, which grow in the higher regions of Colombia.

Propagation is by division when the plant is large enough.

- ☐ Intermediate: 13°C (55°F)
- ☐ Autumn/varied flowering
- ☐ Evergreen/no rest

Right: An intermediate species, Miltonia clowesii mainly flowers in autumn on spikes up to 60cm (2ft) in height.

Miltonia Peach Blossom

This is a typical *Miltonia* hybrid produced from the soft-leaved Colombian species commonly known as the 'pansy orchids'. These hybrids come in a wide variety of colours – white, yellow, pink and red. Peach Blossom is one of the most popular varieties with large, plum red flowers, the colour shading to white towards the edges of the flower.

This orchid and other similar hybrids should be grown in an intermediate greenhouse or a warm room. Their dislike of cold, damp conditions makes them ideally suited to the drier atmosphere in the home. Watering should be on a continuous basis; never allow the plants to dry out completely. The foliage should not be sprayed and feeding should be applied to the pot when watering. One weak feed every three weeks during the spring and summer should be sufficient.

Repotting should be done when the new growth is showing, which may be spring or autumn.

- ☐ Intermediate: 13°C (55°F)
- ☐ Varied flowering season
- ☐ Evergreen/no rest

Below: The fine hybrid Miltonia Peach Blossom can be grown indoors in a warm dry room or in an intermediate greenhouse. It flowers at different times of the year.

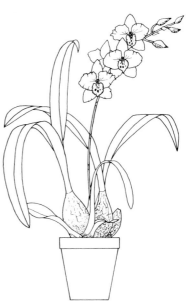

Odontoglossum crispum

Coming from high up in the Andes, this plant needs medium to heavy shade and cool, moist, humid conditions. The large flowers, up to 10cm (4in) across, vary considerably in presence or absence of marking. Flower spikes develop from the side of the new bulb as it is forming and, as the seasons in its native environment are not clearly defined and growth can start at any time, the flowers may open at virtually any time of year, though spring and autumn are probably the most common.

Selective breeding of varieties has been continuing for many years and this has ensured that *Odontoglossum crispum* will still be available to enthusiasts without calling on the dwindling wild stocks; moreover, these cultivated plants are of higher quality. As an ancestor, *Odontoglossum crispum* has probably contributed more towards improving the flower size and shape of *Odontoglossum* and *Odontioda* hybrids than any other species.

Above: Odontoglossum crispum is a cool-house species that flowers at various times of the year, most commonly in spring or autumn. It is a beautiful orchid which comes from high up in the Andes and has long lasting sprays.

☐ Cool: 10°C (50°F)
☐ Varied flowering season
☐ Evergreen/slight rest

Sophronitis coccinea

Although only six species of this miniature epiphytic orchid are known, all of which come from Brazil, it has always been well represented in orchid collections, and its alliance with cattleyas has produced some of the most striking of the intergeneric hybrids.

In their natural habitat these plants grow mainly in areas of high humidity and shade, and therefore are subjects for the cool or intermediate house, with good shade during the summer months. They seem to grow best on a piece of cork bark, but they will also grow in a pot. Perfect drainage at the root is essential. Unfortunately, even in ideal conditions, sophronitis plants seem to have a lifespan of only a few years.

Formerly known as *S. grandiflora*, this orchid is vegetatively similar to a tiny cattleya, growing no higher than 7.5cm (3in). The single flower, 6.5cm (2.6in) across, is produced on a short stem that grows from the top of the pseudobulb. These petals are broader than the sepals and all the segments are bright scarlet, with the lip marked or lined with yellow.

- ☐ Cool/intermediate: 10-13°C (50-55°F)
- ☐ Varied flowering season
- ☐ Evergreen/no rest

Right: Charming flowers appear on Sophronitis coccinea at various times, though mainly during autumn and winter. This miniature, epiphytic orchid suits cool or intermediate conditions, but its lifespan is limited.

Zygopetalum intermedium

This genus comprises 20 species, most of which come from Brazil. They are mainly terrestrial, producing rounded pseudobulbs with long but fairly narrow leaves.

These are ideal plants for the

intermediate house and require good light, with plenty of moisture at the root when in full growth. Air movement around the plant in conditions of high humidity is very important, otherwise the leaves soon become badly spotted; and, for this reason, they should never be sprayed.

Often known as *Z. mackayi*, this plant produces an upright flower spike, 46-60cm (18-24in) in height, from inside the first leaves of a new growth. The spike bears four to eight flowers, each 7.5cm (3in) across. The sepals and petals are of equal size, and bright green blotched with brown. The lip, in contrast, is broad, flat and basically white, heavily lined with purple. These heavily scented flowers last for four or five weeks during the winter months.

☐ Intermediate: 13°C (55°F)
☐ Winter flowering
☐ Evergreen/dry rest

Right: The Zygopetalum intermedium is a fragrant, winter-flowering species for the intermediate house. It thrives in good light with plenty of moisture during growth.

Difficult to Grow

A few orchids are extremely difficult to grow to perfection and those featured in this section are best avoided until you have gained a few years experience at growing the easier ones.

It is not simply the temperature ranges that make these orchids difficult to cultivate – some will present a challenge to your skills irrespective of the conditions you can provide. Indeed, several of the species described here do not necessarily require high temperatures, and others, such as *Huntleya burtii*, are even susceptible to high temperatures and humidity.

Some species in this section, such as *Vanda sanderana*, are now rarely cultivated. This is because they have been used extensively for hybridization and the hybrids have taken over in popularity.

Brassavola digbyana

This is the largest of the genus which, though still horticulturally known as *Brassavola*, is botanically more correctly *Rhyncholaelia digbyana*. In commercial catalogues it can be found under either name.

The lemon-scented flower is incredibly beautiful and contains a deep fringe to the lip, which is a rare occurrence in orchids. The reason for this deeply fimbriated lip is not fully understood, although it is thought to guide or assist the pollinating insect in some way. Usually single flowers are produced which last for up to three weeks.

The plant has been used very extensively in hybridization to produce the large-lipped brassocattleyas etc, although the distinctive shape of the fringe, so characteristic of the species, has never been reproduced to the same extent in its offspring.

The apex of the intermediate greenhouse is an ideal position for this sun-worshipping plant, where it will thrive in the air movement at the roof of the house.

- ☐ Intermediate: 13°C (55°F)
- ☐ Summer flowering
- ☐ Evergreen/dry rest

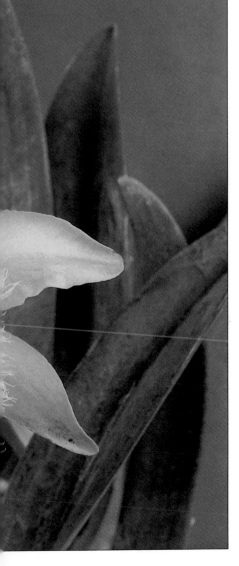

Left: Brassavola digbyana does best in intermediate temperatures. This orchid likes sun but can be shy to flower. Large, single blooms are produced in the summer and frequently last for up to three weeks.

Coelogyne cristata

Perhaps the most familiar of the genus, this species likes to grow on undisturbed into a specimen plant. The flower spike appears from the centre of the new growth and its snowy-white flowers, broken only by a blotch of golden yellow at the centre of the lip, appear from midwinter to early spring.

Although the genus contains well over 100 species, few coelogynes are found in collections today. This is a pity, for they are orchids of great merit. Many species thrive in cool conditions, requiring a warmer environment only during their active growing season. They are a challenge to bloom and must be rested well in winter to achieve flowering.

Many coelogynes are suitable for growing on into specimen plants. However, be warned: a specimen plant of one of the larger-growing species can take up a considerable amount of space in the greenhouse. Fortunately, it is possible to choose from a wide range of smaller-growing species, and even a single-growth plant in flower is a valuable addition to any orchid collection.

- ☐ Cool: 10°C (50°F)
- ☐ Winter/spring flowering
- ☐ Evergreen/dry rest

Left: A delightful species suited for the cool greenhouse, Coelogyne cristata must be rested well to flower regularly.

length. The erect flower spike arises higher up on the bulb than in most cymbidiums, and several spikes are often carried at the same time. The plant is often erratic in its flowering, producing from one to three 7.5cm (3in) flowers to each spike. The flowers, which open in winter and early spring, are white to ivory in colour, with a deep yellow band in the middle of the lip, flanked by two yellow keels.

Very prominent in hybridization, *Cym. eburneum* was one of the parents of the first hybrid cymbidium to be raised in cultivation – Eburneolowianum – which was registered by Veitch in 1889.

Although it is an important species in breeding, the plant does not grow vigorously, and is a shy bloomer. It is now rare and considered a collector's item.

Cymbidium eburneum

Discovered in the 1830s by the botanical explorer William Griffiths, this species is native to the Khasia hills in northern India. It is a compact grower with narrow pseudobulbs, and leaves that can grow to more than 60cm (24in) in

☐ Cool: 10°C (50°F)
☐ Winter/spring flowering
☐ Evergreen/no rest

Below: Cymbidium eburneum is a cool-growing species that produces one to three flowers in the winter and spring months. This orchid is a shy bloomer.

Dendrobium Louisae

A very popular plant, this evergreen hybrid is widely grown and is readily available on both sides of the Atlantic. The plant was raised in Indonesia and resulted from the crossing of two showy species native to New Guinea, *D. phalaenopsis* var. *schroederanum* and *D. veratrifolium*, both of which bear long sprays of rose-mauve flowers. *D*. Louisae combines the characteristics of both parents and produces long arching sprays of flowers from the top of the bulbs. The 6cm (2.4in) flowers, which are a rich rose-purple, are extremely long lived and appear during the autumn and winter. The showy flowers can be used in floral arrangements to good effect. The plant can be grown in a warm sunny room or green-house where it enjoys an abundance of light. Generous growing conditions will produce excellent results.

Propagation is very slow, and not easily achieved from the old canes. The plant should be grown on without division, unless considerably large. Do not overpot. Repot as soon as new growth is seen.

☐ Warm 16-18°C (60-65°F)
☐ Autumn/winter flowering
☐ Evergreen/semi-dry rest

Above: Dendrobium Louisae is a warm-growing, sun-loving hybrid for autumn or winter blooming. It produces arching sprays of long-lasting flowers.

Dendrobium speciosum

A most attractive species from
Australia, this plant enjoys
warmth and humidity during its
growing season, with a decided rest
during the winter. It is not unusual
for this rest period to last for many
months. No water should be given
while the plant is at rest.

If ripened sufficiently the plant will
bloom profusely in the spring,
producing a shower of flower spikes
bearing many rather small, densely
packed flowers, off white in colour
with the lip lightly spotted in purple.
The flowers have a particularly
delightful fragrance.

Not often seen in cultivation, this is
a rewarding plant to grow where
generous conditions permit. It can
attain considerable size and is one of
the largest of the genus, although
slower growing than most. It does
not propagate from old bulbs and
should be grown on to a large plant
and eventually divided. Repot when
new growth is seen.

No hybrids have been produced
from this particular species.

☐ Intermediate/warm:
   13-18°C (55-65°F)
☐ Spring flowering
☐ Evergreen/extended dry rest

*Above: Dendrobium speciosum is an
unusual species that bears a shower
of fragrant blooms in the spring.
Although slow-growing, it eventually
forms a large plant.*

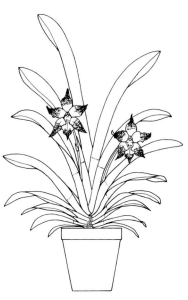

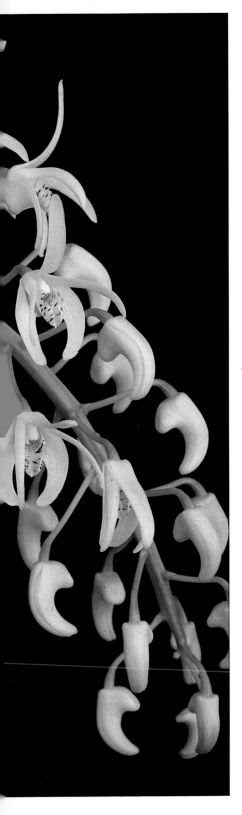

Huntleya burtii

This South American plant grows without pseudobulbs. The leaves, about 30cm (12in) in length, develop from a central stem in the form of a fan. Single flowers 6.5-7.5cm (2.5-3in) across, are produced on a 15cm (6in) stem. The sepals and petals are approximately equal in size and uniform in marking; at the base they are greenish-white, changing through yellow to a reddish-brown marked with yellow. The lower half of the lip is reddish-brown, graduating to white in the upper part. These flowers are thick and waxy in texture and last well.

Huntleya burtii has a reputation for being rather difficult to maintain in good condition, but failure is often due to one of two reasons. The first is that many growers have a tendency to keep the plant in too warm and humid an environment, causing it to rot; the second is that the new growths which develop part way up the stem are often mistakenly removed and repotted. It is far better to allow the plant to grow into a clump, and to let the roots from new growths develop as aerial roots.

- ☐ Intermediate: 13°C (55°F)
- ☐ Summer flowering
- ☐ Evergreen/no rest

Right: The famous 'butterfly orchid', Oncidium papilio, grows in the warm house and flowers at various times. The flowers appear in succession one at a time from the top of a tall slender stem.

Oncidium papilio

Often referred to as the 'butterfly orchid' because of its resemblance to that insect, this species has flowers that open on the end of a long slender stem and sway in the slightest air movement. Only one per stem opens at any one time, but in succession, so that the plant is in flower for many months. The flowers, which can be up to 13cm (5in) across, are a mixture of chestnut brown and yellow.

The plant has squat pseudobulbs each of which supports a solitary, rigid, reddish-green leaf. The plant grows best on a raft suspended from the roof of the warm house, where it will get that little extra bit of light. It should never be kept too wet at the roots, and does best when kept continually on the dry side, relying upon the humidity in the greenhouse for most of its moisture. It should not be overhead sprayed. This is not a plant for growing indoors.

Rare in the wild, the plants seen in cultivation have usually been grown from seed.

- ☐ Warm: 18°C (65°F)
- ☐ Varied flowering season
- ☐ Evergreen/semi-dry rest

Vanda sanderana

A magnificent summer-flowering orchid from the Philippines that grows to about 60cm (2ft) or more in height. The leaves are 30-38cm (12-15in) long, and the flower spikes semi-erect with seven to 20 flowers clustered together. The flowers, 13cm (5in) across, are almost flat, with the upper sepal soft rose to white in colour suffused with whitish-pink, and the lower sepals round, slightly larger, and tawny yellow crossed with red markings. The petals are smaller than the sepals and are white to rose coloured with red blotches near the base; the lip is tawny yellow, streaked with red. Although this species adjusts to varying conditions and will, if necessary, tolerate some coolness, it generally grows best in warmth and sun.

This species has been used extensively for the breeding of quality hybrids and is the pedigree of most modern *Vanda* hybrids. However, the species is today quite rare and is seldom seen in cultivation in the western world.

- ☐ Warm: 18°C (65°F)
- ☐ Summer flowering
- ☐ Evergreen/semi-rest

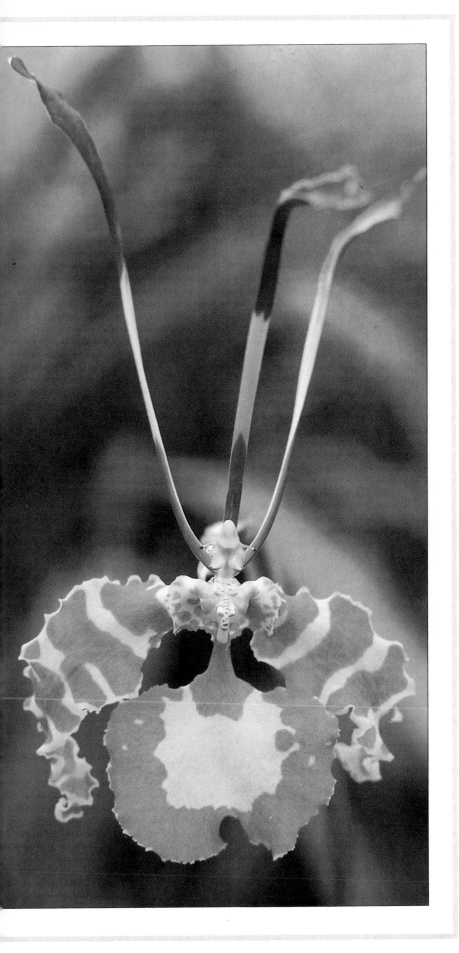

Above: Long, dense sprays of small flowers adorn the intermediate species Rhynchostylis retusa during the winter and spring. However, the blooms last for only two or three weeks.

Index

A
Ada aurantiaca 15
Aerides fieldingii 63
Angraecum eburneum 16
Angraecum sesquipedale 17
Anguloa clowesii 18
Aphid 12

B
Bifrenaria harrisoniae 19
Brassavola 62
Brassavola digbyana 85
Brassavola nodosa 69
Brassia verrucosa 20
Brassolaeliocattleya Crusader 21
Brassolaeliocattleya Queen Elizabeth 21
Brown spot 12
Bulbophyllum collettii 22
Butterfly orchid 92
Buttonholes 11

C
Calanthe vestita 23
Cattleya 12-14, 21, 24-26, 42, 62, 76, 82
Cattleya aurantiaca 24, 76
Cattleya bowringiana 25
Cattleya forbesii 26
Chysis bractescens 69
Clown orchid 49
Coelogyne cristata 87
Compost, advice on 8
Containers, advice on 10-11
Corsages 11
Cradle orchid 18
Cymbidium 27-31, 88
Cymbidium Angelica 'Advent' 27
Cymbidium Ayres Rock 'Cooksbridge Velvet' 28
Cymbidium Baltic 29
Cymbidium Cariga 30
Cymbidium devonianum 31
Cymbidium eburneum 88
Cymbidium Fort George 'Lewes' 29
Cymbidium Lucense 27
Cymbidium Lucy Moor 27
Cymbidium Mission Bay 31
Cymbidium mosaic virus 13
Cymbidium Putana 30
Cymbidium Stonehaven 'Cooksbridge' 30
Cymbidium Touchstone 'Janis' 31
Cymbidium York Meredith 29

D
Deciduous orchids 8
Dendrobium 11, 32-35, 70-71, 89-90

Dendrobium album 35
Dendrobium aureum 32
Dendrobium densiflorum 32-33
Dendrobium Gatton Sunray 70
Dendrobium heterocarpum 32
Dendrobium Louisae 89
Dendrobium nobile 34
Dendrobium phalaenopsis var. *schroederanum* 89
Dendrobium speciosum 90
Dendrobium strebloceras 71
Dendrobium superbum 35
Dendrobium Tangerine 'Tillgates' 71
Dendrobium veratrifolium 89
Disease 12-13
Display, advice on 10-11
Doritis pulcherrima 72

E
Encyclia cochleata 36
Encyclia mariae 73
Encyclia vitellina 37
Epidendrum ibaguense 38-39
Epidendrum radicans 38-39
Epidendrum stamfordianum 40
Epiphytic orchids 6, 8-9, 15, 18-20, 41, 43, 59, 63-66, 69, 82
Evergreen orchids 8

F
Feeding, advice on 9
Flowers, anatomy of 7
Foxtail orchid 63

G
Gastrochilus acutifolius 64
Gomeza crispa 41
Grammangis ellisii 74
Greenfly 12
Griffiths, William 88

H
Humidity 9-10
Huntleya burtii 84, 91

I
Infestation, advice on 12-13
Insecticide 12

L
Laelia 14, 21, 42, 62, 68, 74-76
Laelia anceps 42
Laelia cinnabarina 68, 74-75
Laelia Coronet 76
Laeliocattleya Chitchat 'Tangerine' 76
Laeliocattleya Trivanhoe 21
Lily of the valley orchid 50
Lithophytic 69